MW01290413

7 Visions 7 Truths

The Book of Revelation

Seven Truths from God that will change your life forever!

outskirtspress

DENVER, COLORADO

The opinions expressed in this manuscript are solely the opinions of the author and do not represent the opinions or thoughts of the publisher. The author has represented and warranted full ownership and/or legal right to publish all the materials in this book.

All scripture quotations, unless otherwise indicated, are taken from the Holy Bible, New International Version®, NIV®. Copyright ©1973, 1978, 1984, 2011 by Biblica, Inc.™ Used by permission of Zondervan. All rights reserved worldwide. www.zondervan.com The "NIV" and "New International Version" are trademarks registered in the United States Patent and Trademark Office by Biblica, Inc.™

The "NIV" trademarks are registered in the United States Patent and Trademark Office by International Bible Society. Use of either trademark requires the permission of the International Bible Society.

7 Visions 7 Truths
The Book of Revelation: Seven truths from God that will change your life forever.
All Rights Reserved.
Copyright © 2014 Rev. David Scherbarth
v3.0

Cover Photo © 2014 Rev. David Scherbarth. All rights reserved - used with permission.

This book may not be reproduced, transmitted, or stored in whole or in part by any means, including graphic, electronic, or mechanical without the express written consent of the publisher except in the case of brief quotations embodied in critical articles and reviews.

Outskirts Press, Inc.
http://www.outskirtspress.com

ISBN: 978-1-4787-3390-4

Outskirts Press and the "OP" logo are trademarks belonging to Outskirts Press, Inc.

PRINTED IN THE UNITED STATES OF AMERICA

Table of Contents

Preface

The Seven Messages in the Revelation

The book of Revelation is a book of pictures. There are seven major visions within the Revelation and eight lesser visions which supplement the major visions. Within those pictures or visions God reveals seven truths that explain the world we live in and that also reveal the future. Using images of calamity and savage beasts and horrible pictures of dragons and loss, God tells the story of what will happen and why it will happen. God wrote the Revelation to reveal the future to all people living between the first and the second coming of Jesus. I invite you to take a walk with me through the art gallery that is the Revelation. I will show you the seven messages God has embedded in these visions. This is a walk that will change your life.

I am Reverend David Scherbarth. For the past forty years I have been a pastor in Christian churches large and small. More importantly, I have been teaching the Bible for forty years. I am eager to share with you the lessons that forty years of Bible study in the book of the Revelation have taught me. Together we will look at each of the visions God drew in the Revelation and I will help you discover the seven messages God has placed within these visions. When you have finished your walk through these pictures, you will understand the lessons God wants you to learn.

God wrote every word of the Bible. As such, the entire Bible is valuable to learn and study. But, that said, the book of Revelation stands apart for New Testament Christians. God had a very special purpose in mind when he wrote this book. As God put it in the first verse of Revelation, *The revelation of Jesus Christ, which God gave him to show his servants what must soon take place.* (Rev. 1:1 NIV) God wrote this book to reveal the future. God has a plan for this world. In the Revelation God explains his plan and shows us how he is carrying it out. It is fair to say, given the stated purpose God had in writing the Revelation, that no book of the Bible is more important for New Testament Christians to read and to understand than the book of Revelation.

But there is a problem. *"No one can understand the book of Revelation."* This is the common consensus of the majority of people in this world regarding the visions in Revelation. Maybe you are part of that majority opinion. It is easy to understand why people think this. Bible scholars have struggled for centuries to understand what the Revelation teaches. These men and women of learning have expended much energy trying to comprehend the Revelation's messages. They have poured over the pictures God created. They have compared the images in the visions to the ancient Old Testament texts upon which many of the images are founded. They have studied historical events and compared them to the Revelation to see if they could discern a pattern. They have applied their reason and, failing that, their prodigious imaginations, to understand what the Lord wrote. Thousands of years of study! Hundreds of thousands of pages written to explain the Revelation! And what is the result of this immense effort? Confusion! The more people have tried to explain the pictures in the Revelation, the more the confusion has grown. In the end people, Christians and unbelievers alike, have come to one solid conclusion. *"No one can understand the book of Revelation."*

Until now! You will not find any of that confusion as you walk with me through the visions of the Revelation. Together we will not only uncover the messages contained within each of the pictures. We will also find that God's messages will change our lives. This is the expectation I want you to have as you read this book. You will achieve three specific goals.

First of all, once you have finished your journey, you will understand the message of the Revelation. In fact, you will understand the Revelation so well, that you will be able to explain it to other people. And, surprisingly, you will find this study of the Revelation to be easier than you thought it would be. I know that this claim may sound impossible to your ears. How could you possibly expect to easily understand the message God has placed in his visions when so many others have found only confusion? The answer lies in the approach to the visions which you will learn in this book. The Revelation is a book of pictures. We do not approach a picture the way we approach a book when we seek to learn the meaning of each one. We will learn to look at each vision in the Revelation as we would look at a picture, using picture reading skills to discern the meaning of the pictures God paints. What you will find is that each vision contains a message from God. Learning these messages and putting them together will open a whole new view of the world around you.

This brings us to the second thing you will gain from this walk. Armed with what you learn from the Revelation, you will be able to understand what is happening in the world around you. Our five senses tell us that the world seems to be governed by chaos. There seems to be no rhyme or reason for the horrific events that occur almost daily. The truths of the Revelation will open your eyes to a pattern. There is a God and that God has a plan for this world. God is carrying out his plan right now through all the events that are happening in this world. In the Revelation God explains his plan and he shows us why things happen as they do. Once you know and understand what God teaches in the Revelation, you will be equipped to read the newspaper and to listen to the nightly news with an understanding you never thought possible. You will see that even the most horrible events will fit into God's plan and serve his purpose.

Finally, when you finish your walk through the gallery of pictures that is the Revelation, your life will be changed. The truths you learn from the Revelation will equip you to live in this world with hope and confidence. Your life is not an accident. God has a reason for giving you each new day and a purpose for you to fulfill. You will discover that purpose as you learn the truths of the Revelation and it will change your life.

There is one more thing we must recognize before we begin our walk together. When it comes to the book of Revelation, the world divides into two clear groups. One group approaches the Revelation in unbelief. These people see the visions depicting wars and famines and earthquakes and death and destruction, and their hearts are filled with fear. Each frightening image carries a message of judgment from the God of heaven, and that is exactly what God intends for them. God uses each new catastrophe pictured in the Revelation to warn the unbelievers in this world that now is the time to repent, before a greater Day of Judgment comes upon them.

But there is a second group of people in this world when it comes to reading the Revelation, and I hope you join me in this group. This group reads the Revelation with faith in their hearts. As these Christians read the Revelation, they are able to look past the dragons and beasts and wars. For them the visions carry promises from God to sustain them and to protect them every day on this earth. They embrace the assurances from the Lord that one day they will experience the full victory God has won for them in heaven through faith in Jesus Christ. As God equips them with his promises, they find comfort and strength for each new day on this earth. As you walk through the visions of this special book, walk in faith and listen for the comforting promises of God.

CHAPTER ONE
Equipping Ourselves to Read the Revelation

Learning the Three Bible Reading Principles

Before we begin reading the Revelation, we must first prepare ourselves for the task. The Revelation requires special Bible reading skills if we are going to understand the messages God is revealing through the pictures painted in this book. These skills are important for all Bible reading, but they are especially needed for reading Revelation.

Over the years of my ministry I have met thousands of Christians, and I have found one thing to be fairly consistent in all of them. Just about every Christian I have met intends to read the entire Bible sometime in his life. Many, perhaps even most, have attempted to do that very thing. However the sad truth is, while many have attempted to read the Bible from cover to cover, most have failed to do so. They tried and then they quit. When I asked these Christians why they did not complete the task, all of them gave some form of the same answer. They said the problem was the Bible. It was too confusing. It was too hard to understand.

Unfortunately, their analysis of the experience is not correct. The problem is not the Bible. The problem is that they lacked the necessary Bible reading skills. The first step in acquiring those skills is to learn the three *"Bible Reading Principles"* that must guide the study of God's word. Once you know these three principles, not only will you find that you can read the Bible, you will actually find that the Bible is surprisingly easy to understand.

The First Bible Reading Principle is this. *"The Bible is a simple book, clear in its meaning!"* When God wrote the Bible, he said what he meant and he meant what he said. God wrote every word in the Bible, and he chose each word intentionally. God is saying exactly what he meant to say. Therefore, as we read the Bible, we must first pay attention to the words God chose. We must strive to understand the words as they are written. We do not need to seek some deeper "hidden" meaning beneath the words. God wrote exactly what he meant, so our first task is to understand his words as he wrote them. When God tells us that the Israelites crossed the Red Sea on dry land, we will understand that this is exactly what happened. When God says Daniel emerged safely after spending a night in a den filled with hungry lions, we know this happened exactly in this way. If God says that a given segment of the Bible is a "vision" or a "parable," we will understand that section to be what God says it is. Throughout the Bible, the first approach is always to understand God to mean exactly what his words say.

When you apply this principle to your reading of the Bible, you will find that the book becomes clear, even simple to understand. In fact, it becomes so clear that even a fourth grade child, someone who has just learned how to read, can read the Bible and understand what he is reading. Now I know! You are already thinking that this bold statement cannot be true. It expresses a thought that is much different from your own experience reading God's word. So let me give you an example to show you how this principle works.

In the book of Exodus God tells us how long it took him to create the universe. *For in six days the LORD made the heavens and the earth, the sea, and all that is in them, but he rested on the seventh day.* (Ex. 20:11 NIV) Look closely at the words in this verse. Every word in this verse is a simple word. Even a fourth grade child could put all these words together and understand exactly what God is saying. God tells us in very simple and clear language that he created the universe in six days. These words are very clear. There is no ambiguity or confusion in that statement, right?

Yet, here is the thing. While God clearly says this, the majority of people in our world do not believe it. The problem is not that the Bible is unclear or confusing. The problem is that in this world people do not want to accept what God is saying. For this reason when they encounter this passage, some people try to change what God is saying as they *"seek a deeper meaning"* in his words, one with which they are more comfortable. The problem is not that God failed to clearly say what he meant. The problem is that people at times do not want to accept what God says, so they try to alter it. If we are going to avoid this error, we must apply the First Principle of Bible Reading. As we read the book of Revelation, our first step will always be to understand the words as God wrote them. We can always trust God to clearly say what he means.

This brings us to the Second Principle of Bible Reading. *"The Bible interprets itself."* Many people think that in order to understand what God says in the Bible, you have to "interpret" the things God says. They assume what is needed here is an active imagination that can find hidden ideas beneath the words God wrote to uncover what God is really teaching. Using this approach, people have a tendency to make the Bible say whatever they want it to say, rather than to understand what God is saying. As you might expect from such an approach, this leads to the confusion we see in this world when it comes to understanding the Bible.

The problem that causes this confusion is that people are not applying the Second Principle of Bible Reading, namely, that the Bible interprets itself. The Bible is a unique book. God designed the Bible in such a way that the Bible explains itself. What we read in one place in the Bible, God will explain in another part of the Bible when writing on the same subject. Therefore we can rely on God to explain what he means by simply reading what he said elsewhere in the book. We will not have to supply our own guesses or employ our imagination to invent a meaning for what God wrote. We will not need a special skill to interpret the Bible. God already did that for us. The Bible interprets itself.

We are going to make much use of this principle as we read the Revelation. First we will look at the visions God draws. When the images are difficult to understand, we will look elsewhere in the Bible to see if God has drawn these same pictures before. Often we will find that God has not only used these pictures before, he also explains what the pictures mean. In this way God will reveal the meaning of the Revelation visions. The Bible interprets itself.

There are some people who object to the Second Principle of Bible Reading. They say you can't rely on the Bible to interpret itself because they say the Bible contradicts itself. This is where we employ the Third Principle of Bible Reading. *"The Bible never contradicts itself."* Let me state that fact again because it is critical to our Bible reading success. The Bible NEVER contradicts itself. What God says in one place in the Bible, he confirms everywhere else in the Bible. God never contradicts himself and we must be careful not to do so either.

Suppose, for example, we read a given passage from Scripture and derive a given meaning from the words we read. Then we read another passage in the Bible and we find that our understanding of the previous passage contradicts what God clearly says in the second passage. At that point we know that we are wrong in our first understanding. We must start again. God never contradicts himself. What he states in one place, he fully confirms everywhere else. We must make sure in our Bible reading that we honor that principle. The Bible never contradicts itself.

These are the three Bible reading principles: the Bible is a simple book, clear in its meaning; the Bible interprets itself; and the Bible never contradicts itself. We must have them clearly in mind when we read any part of the Bible, and we will make ample use of them as we read the book of Revelation. These principles will enable us to understand the message God has embedded within the visions of the Revelation.

The Timeframe of the Revelation Visions

Understanding the timeframe of the Revelation is also critical to our preparation. If we are going to comprehend God's message, we will need to have a very clear understanding of what period of earth history the visions are describing. From the very first words of the Revelation, it is obvious that there is an urgency to our study. God informs us of that urgency with the first words he records in this book: *The revelation of Jesus Christ, which God gave him to show his servants what must soon take place.* (Rev. 1:1 NIV) God tells us he wrote this book to show his servants what was about to happen in this world. God is going to reveal the future. God wants us to understand our world and to be prepared for what is coming. He focuses our attention on *"what must soon take place."*

As with so many things in this world, even simple statements like *"what must soon take place"* can cause confusion in people's minds. Some people think that God is about to describe what will happen in the time of John. Others say that is not correct. They say that this phrase refers to what will happen in the time just before the end of the world. The fact is, neither one of these assumptions is correct. If either one of these assumptions were correct, God would be writing something that had no application for almost all New Testament Christians. Secondly, if we try to apply either one of these assumptions to the visions of the Revelation, we will find the visions don't match the context.

There is a better and simpler understanding of the phrase *"what must soon take place."* With this phrase God is speaking of the entire New Testament era. This is the timeframe of the Revelation. We are led to this conclusion by statements within the Revelation. For example, there are a number of references in Revelation which lead us to associate the beginning of the timeframe with the completion of Jesus' ministry on this earth.

Jesus begins Revelation by identifying himself with the phrase *"the firstborn from the dead."* This title is based on the fact that Jesus rose from the dead on Easter Sunday. Now he awaits the resurrection of all people at the end of time. To identify himself in this way indicates that the event of the resurrection happened before Jesus revealed the visions of the future. This marks the resurrection of Jesus as a starting point for the visions in the Revelation.

A supporting time reference occurs in Revelation chapters four and five. There Jesus invites John into heaven where he witnesses a huge celebration. They are celebrating the return of the Lamb to heaven after he *"has been slain."* This is a picture of Ascension Day as we will see when we study that chapter. The ascended Lamb then begins to open the seals and the future God is revealing begins to unfold. Therefore the beginning point of the visions in Revelation coincides with this act by the risen Savior.

There is one more vision within the Revelation that helps us to fix the time when the visions begin. That vision God records in Revelation chapter 20. There God reveals at the beginning of the *"thousand years"* he will bind Satan and limit his power. We will learn that God is drawing another picture of the New Testament era with this picture of a *"thousand years,"* meaning that Satan will be bound for the majority of this timeframe. That "binding" is done by the chain of the Gospel, as we will see when we study chapter twenty. It coincides with the Gospel message filling the world after Jesus' ascension into heaven. This too leads us to fix the time when the visions begin as coinciding with the first coming of Jesus.

The end of the timeframe of the Revelation is pictured in the visions themselves. Generally the visions in the Revelation end with one of three events: the last days just before the Lord's return describing the final battle between the forces of God and the forces of Satan; the

Judgment Day itself marking Jesus' return to destroy the world with fire; or the final judgment before God's throne in heaven. Therefore we can identify the end of the timeframe in Revelation as the time of Jesus' return.

Taken together we have a beginning point and an ending point for each vision in the Revelation. Every single vision begins with the first coming of Christ and ends with the second coming of Christ. Each vision reveals a truth that applies to that entire period of time. If we are going to understand the visions God reveals in the book of Revelation, we must keep this timeframe firmly in mind. Only when we see the visions in this context will we understand their meaning.

The Outline of the Revelation

Since the truths God teaches are presented in a series of progressive thoughts, each new one built upon the one that precedes it, we also need a general understanding of the outline of the visions of the Revelation. We begin with chapter one which serves as the introduction to the book. Following this we will study the first section of the Revelation which contains the Vision of the Seven Letters. After this we will study the Vision of the Seven Seals. Then the Vision of the Seven Trumpets. Then the Vision of the Seven Visions. Then the Vision of the Seven Bowls of Wrath. I hope you are noticing the number seven here! We will conclude our study with the Vision of the Judgment of God's Enemies and the Three Visions of Heaven. In all there are seven visions which comprise the book of Revelation.

From the outline we can begin to see that God repeats certain numbers in the Revelation to convey meaning as well. If we are going to understand the Revelation, besides knowing the timeframe of the visions, we also will have to have some understanding of how God uses these numbers and what he means by them. That is the final skill we now must acquire. Once we accomplish that task, we will be ready to begin our study of the book of Revelation.

Chapter Summary

Our plan is to employ the Three Bible Reading Principles as we read the book of Revelation:

Principle One: *The Bible is a simple book, clear in its meaning!* God meant what he said and he said what he meant, choosing each word of the Bible carefully. For this reason our first step in reading the Revelation will be to understand the words as God wrote them. We will not look for any deeper hidden meaning or attempt to supply our own imaginative guesses as to what a given word or image might mean. We will take God at his word and we will let God guide us to the meaning he wants us to find.

Principle Two: *The Bible interprets itself!* When we encounter difficult images or pictures in the Revelation, we will search the rest of the Bible to see if God used these same pictures in other places. Often we will find that God not only has previously used these images, but in those places in the Bible God has also explained the meaning behind them. Therefore we will use the Bible to explain the Bible.

Principle Three: *The Bible never contradicts itself!* What God says in one place in the Bible, he confirms everywhere else in the Bible when he speaks on the same topic. For this reason we will be careful to make sure that any insight we gain from a given passage does not contradict what God clearly says elsewhere in the Bible. God agrees with himself in all he wrote. We will make sure that we follow that same approach.

The Timeframe of the Revelation: *God wrote the Revelation to reveal what will happen on this earth between the first coming of Jesus and the second coming of Jesus. Every vision in the Revelation begins and ends with those time markers. Any truth God reveals in a given vision will apply to that entire period of time and all who live in any age between the first and the second coming of Christ will see that truth occur in their lives.*

CHAPTER TWO
Understanding the Numbers of the Revelation

There is only one thing left to do to complete our preparation. That one thing has to do with the numbers which God repeats in the book of Revelation. This may be the hardest part of our preparation and we should spend some time with it to get a clear understanding. As we turn our attention to this topic, perhaps a couple of words are in order.

I have told you that it is not my plan or method to supply interpretations or guesses for anything God presents in the Revelation. Generally, we will follow the three principles of Bible reading. We will take God's words as he wrote them. We will accept what God chooses to explain. And when something in the Revelation is not explained, we will accept that, and wait for the Lord himself to explain it on Judgment Day. All this is true, generally speaking, until we come to the repeating numbers in the Revelation. Here we encounter a problem.

In the book of Revelation God repeats four numbers over and over again. They are the numbers seven, three and one-half, twelve, and ten. God repeats these numbers so often that it is obvious he is telling us something with them. The problem is, nowhere in the Revelation or in the rest of the Bible, does God explain the message behind each number. There is no passage in the Bible where God says, *"I used the number seven in the Revelation and here is the message I am sending by its use."* This leaves us with an unexplained issue.

Normally we would simply leave this matter as it stands and wait for the Lord to clearly reveal its meaning on the Last Day. However, since God repeats these numbers so often, the constant repetition seems to indicate that the meaning these numbers carry will be vital to our understanding of the visions. Therefore, based on that assumption, it is necessary that we take a closer look at how God uses the numbers to see if we can learn the message God attaches to them. That is what we are going to do here. To accomplish this, we will employ this methodology. We will compare the different uses of each number and look for a pattern. What we are looking for is "common ground." Our hope is that this will lead to an understanding of God's message within each number. We begin with the number seven.

The Number "Seven"

Seven is the most common number God repeats in the Revelation. Starting in chapter one, we encounter the number seven as God introduces the Holy Spirit. God calls him the "seven spirits" of God who are before the throne of heaven. This is a very unusual name for the Holy Spirit. Only Revelation uses this term "seven spirits" of God. Therefore we can see that God attaches the number seven to the Holy Spirit.

At the end of chapter one, when God shows us the Vision of Christ Among the Lampstands, we encounter the church of God. God draws the picture of seven individual lampstands in the vision. He tells us the seven lampstands are the seven churches of God. So now we find God applying the number seven to the visible church.

We read on in Revelation until we come to chapter five. There we encounter the number seven again, this time in connection with the future of this world. In the vision we see the God of heaven and earth seated on a throne in heaven on Ascension Day. In his hand is a scroll, and the scroll contains the future of the world. The problem is that the scroll is sealed and there are seven seals. So we have the number seven attached to the future of the world on Ascension Day.

As chapter five unfolds we encounter the number seven one more time. A Lamb appears looking *"as though it had been slain,"* a clear reference to Jesus after his death and resurrection. This Lamb has seven horns and seven eyes. So we find God attaches the number seven to Jesus Christ.

We have four different entities: the Holy Spirit, the church, the future of the world and Jesus Christ. To all of them God attaches the number seven. It is as if God is telling us that these four different entities are all connected in some important way. Our question would be, "What is it that connects them?" It will most likely surprise you to learn that you already know the answer. It lies in the most well known passage in the Bible. *For God so loved the world that he gave his one and only Son, that whoever believes in him shall not perish but have eternal life.* (John 3:16 NIV) We call this passage the Gospel. It contains the "covenant" or "promise" of God that he will provide salvation for all mankind and whoever believes in Jesus will be saved. Each of the four things attached to the number seven has a clear connection to this Gospel promise or covenant.

As we look at the Gospel promise God made, we can easily see the connection it has with Jesus. Jesus is the foundation of that promise, the one who created it with his life, death and resurrection. At the same time, we can just as easily see the connection between the Gospel promise and the church. The people of the church are the ones who believe the promise of God, trusting Jesus as their Savior, and through that faith they take part in the Gospel Covenant. So it is very clear that the Gospel Covenant connects both Jesus and the church.

Now we come to the Holy Spirit. He too plays a major role in the establishment of that covenant. The Holy Spirit has a very special job to perform. His job is to create faith. God defines that task in the book of 1 Corinthians. ... *no one can say, "Jesus is Lord," except by the*

Holy Spirit. (1 Cor. 12:3 NIV) So we understand that the Holy Spirit is the one who creates the faith in the hearts of believers. He is the *"covenant maker."* Without his work people could not take part in the covenant through faith.

That leaves one last relationship to connect with the covenant, perhaps the best one of all. The Gospel Covenant established by the Lord is connected directly to the future of the world. We might at first wonder what possible connection can there be between the future and God's covenant promise of the Gospel. It is actually more obvious than we might at first assume. The answer lies in a common question most of us have had as we examine what happens in this world. So often the news of this world proclaims the terrible atrocities, the horrible examples of evil which seem to occur on a daily basis. At such moments we wonder why a good and loving and holy God would allow this evil rebellious world to continue. Why doesn't God simply end this world right now?

God answers that question in the Revelation. He says, *"I know your question. Here is the answer, the number seven!"* It stands for the Gospel Covenant. Remember the vision of Ascension Day in Revelation chapter five. God held the scroll containing the future of the world. That future was marked with seven seals. As God opened one seal after another, the future of this world unfolded. God attaches the number seven to that process to remind us that what we are seeing, and what we will experience in the future, is about the Gospel Covenant. Each new day God is reaching out to people with the message of hope and light in Christ, before it is too late. This is why God allows the world to continue from one day to the next. This is God's important covenant work! Even though we will see terrible and evil things happening in this world spreading great pain and suffering, we must always remember the number seven. God is reminding us when he uses that number that all things, even the most terrible things, have some role to play in God's good and gracious plan to reach souls in darkness with the message of salvation through Jesus. Seven is the number God uses to remind us of that comfort.

When we put all this together, we understand God uses the number seven to remind us of the message of the Gospel Covenant in the Revelation. When God tells us there are seven letters to seven churches, he wants us to keep in mind that while these churches are at times damaged and hindered by the darkness, God is still using them to carry out his covenant work of the Gospel. When God tells us that there are seven seals, he is reminding us that, even though some of the images in the vision reveal acts of terror and hardship, even these terrible things will play a role in accomplishing the greater good of the Gospel Covenant. Therefore the number seven in the Revelation reminds us of the Gospel Covenant and the important work that God is accomplishing every day.

The Number "Three and One-Half"

Once we understand the message behind the number seven, this understanding opens the way to gain an understanding of the next important repeating number in the Revelation, the number three and one-half. Taken together, these two numbers open our eyes to see the spiritual pattern behind all that happens in this world.

We first encounter the number three and one-half in Revelation chapter eleven. There John is told to measure the Temple, which he does. The Temple in this vision is a picture of the New Testament visible church of God. This Temple is divided into two sections, the inner court which John measures, and the outer court which John is commanded not to measure. God explains the command saying that the outer court of his Temple will be trampled on by the *"gentiles."* The *"gentiles"* in this picture represent "unbelievers, opponents of God." In this vision God is revealing that we will see these opponents of God occupy a large portion of his visible church in this world. This occupation will last for *"42 months."* Here 42 months is the number three and one-half, or three years and six months.

As chapter eleven continues we encounter the number three and one-half again. Two witnesses appear in a vision. They testify to the message of God's light. Even though the dark world objects to their message and wants nothing to do with it, these witnesses keep testifying. They do this for a time period of *"1260 days."* That is the number three and one-half again. It measures three years and six months. John is counting months according to the Jewish calendar which measures months by the movement of the moon. By that measure each month has 30 days.

Then in chapter twelve God applies the number three and one-half to the woman who represents the faithful church of God. It measures her time on this earth and details the persecution and opposition she will encounter until Jesus returns. As the Dragon tries to destroy this woman, God carries her away to a safe place in the wilderness for *"1260 days."* All the while the devil and his forces oppose the church and her work, God keeps her safe.

Putting all this together we find the "common ground" that connects the three examples. That common ground is "rebellion against God." In each case God uses this number to measure the time between the first and the second coming of Christ. When God attaches the number three and one-half to this period of earth history, he is calling our attention to the rebellion that is taking place during this time. The *"gentiles"* were rebelling against God when they overran the Temple. The world was rebelling against God when they opposed the Two Witnesses. The Dragon was rebelling against God when he pursued the Woman in the wilderness. From this we learn that wherever God uses the number three and one-half in the Revelation, he is always measuring a time of rebellion.

Notice that the number three and one-half is half of the number seven. If seven is the number of the Gospel Covenant in the Revelation, then three and one-half is the number of the Broken Covenant. It reminds us that the people of this world love the darkness instead of the light and therefore they rebel against God's covenant. They will live in rebellion against God until Jesus returns and all of us will see that rebellion, no matter what age in which we live. For this reason the Revelation becomes the story of the consequences people will face for daring to rebel against God. Whenever we see the number three and one-half in the Revelation, God wants us to call to mind that he is revealing the consequences people face for rebellion against his covenant in this world.

When you put these two numbers together you have an explanation for all that you see happening in the world around you. Seven, the number of the Gospel Covenant, reminds us that God is doing the urgent work of reaching out with his saving message before it is too late. At the same time, three and one-half, the number of the Broken Covenant, reminds us that God is revealing his wrath toward all who dare to rebel against him as they cling to the darkness. These two numbers explain all that we see around us in this world.

The Number "Twelve"

The third repeating number in the Revelation is the number twelve. Again we look for some "common ground" that connects the uses of the number twelve and its multiples in the Revelation. The number twelve appears in the Revelation in various multiples such as 24 or 144. For example, in Revelation chapter four John sees the throne of God surrounded by 24 other thrones on which are seated 24 elders. The woman in chapter twelve who represents the faithful church of God has a crown with 12 stars, representing the twelve tribes of the Old Testament. When we see the picture of the New Jerusalem in Revelation chapters twenty-one and twenty-two, a picture representing God's church in heaven, the number twelve is everywhere. The city has 12 foundations with 12 gates marked with the names of the 12 apostles, and 12 different precious stones comprise the building materials.

The "common ground" that links each repetition of the number twelve to all the others becomes obvious when we examine each occurrence. Everywhere God uses the number twelve in the Revelation, he associates that number with the church. Sometimes God uses the number twelve to alert readers to the fact that he is about to make a promise to his people. Other times God uses the number twelve to indicate that he is about to fulfill a promise he made to his people. From this association we understand that in the Revelation the number twelve is the number of the church of God.

The book of Revelation makes it plain that we must through much tribulation enter into the kingdom of God. The people of God will always face great danger in this world. We carry the light of God in a world that hates that light. But God does not want his people to live in fear. Therefore throughout the Revelation, God constantly reassures his people of his care and protection and of the final victory he has prepared for them. This is the message God attaches to the number twelve. It is the number of the Church of God. Whenever God uses this number or one of its multiples, God wants us to call to mind the promises of care and protection he makes to his people. Even though we live in a world filled with danger, all is well, for God's promises keep us safe.

The Number "Ten"

The number ten is the final number which God repeats in the Revelation. Again we look for "common ground" to help us understand the message God wants us to remember when he uses this number. We find the first occurrence of the number ten in chapter two. There God announces to the people of the church of Smyrna that they will face a future of persecution for *"10 days."* Ten occurs again in Revelation chapter twelve where we are told that the great Dragon has *"10 horns."* In Revelation chapter thirteen the Beast of the Sea has *"10 horns"* and wears *"10 crowns."* In Revelation chapter seventeen God warns us that the horns on the Beast of the Sea are a metaphor picturing *"10 kings"* who will one day come and will rule for a combined total of *"10 hours."* We also find the number ten in multiple forms. The number 144,000 is a combination of multiples of the numbers twelve squared and ten cubed. And the famous *"1000 years"* of Revelation chapter twenty is the number ten cubed.

As we examine these different uses of the number ten, the "common ground" becomes clear. In each instance, God is expressing the idea of *"completeness."* The church at Smyrna faces a "complete" future filled with continual persecution. The *"10 horns"* of the Dragon and the beast represent complete power on this earth. The *"10 kings"* ruling for a combined *"10 hours"* represent a complete future that believers can expect to see. Christians will see governments using their ruling power to stand against God's covenant plan until Jesus returns. When God combines the square of twelve with the cube of ten to form 144,000, he is picturing his complete church. And when God reveals the *"thousand year kingdom of the Lord"* he is revealing that, during the vast majority of the New Testament, Christ and his saints will rule and Satan will be bound. As we put all this together we find the Lord uses the number ten to remind us of the concept of completeness.

These are the repeating numbers in the Revelation and these are the meanings we can gain from them as God repeats them. Seven is the number of the Gospel Covenant. God uses this number to remind us that what we are seeing in the given pictures somehow plays a role in God's overall plan to reach the world with his Gospel message before it is too late. Three and one-half is the number of the Broken Covenant. It pictures the truth that this world lives in constant rebellion against God and his plan of salvation through faith in Jesus. For this reason we will see examples of God's judgment every day as a natural consequence of this continued rebellion. Twelve is the number of the church. God uses it to remind us of the promises he makes and the promises he keeps to his church. These promises assure God's people that they are secure even as they walk through a very dangerous world. God has promised to watch over them. Ten is the number of completeness reminding us that the visions to which they are attached represent a complete experience we can expect.

These numbers are important to understand as we read the Revelation. They bring comfort to our hearts and they explain what we are seeing. God does not use these numbers by accident or without intent. Each time we encounter one of these repeating numbers, we must actively call to mind the message behind the number. In the context of that number we will find new meaning for the pictures we are studying.

Chapter Summary

Seven is the Number of the Gospel Covenant. *God uses this number in the Revelation to remind us of the important work he is doing each day in this world, reaching people with the message of forgiveness through faith in Jesus before it is too late. When we encounter this number in the Revelation, God wants us to realize that whatever we are seeing in any given vision, even the most terrible sights, somehow have a place in his plan to reach people with his Gospel light.*

Three and One-Half is the Number of the Broken Covenant. *God uses this number in the Revelation to remind us of the fact that many in this world live in open rebellion against God. For this reason, even as God is reaching out with his Gospel message, he at the same time is forced to display his wrath against those who reject his light. Any time we encounter this number in one of its forms, God wants us to call to mind the fact that what we are seeing in the vision is a warning from God to the unbelievers to repent now before a greater judgment comes upon them.*

Twelve is the Number of the Church of God. *God uses the number twelve and its multiples to represent his church in the Revelation. When we see this number or one of its multiples, God wants us to note that in the vision we are studying, he is either making a promise to his church or he is keeping a promise to his church.*

Ten is the Number of Completeness. *God uses the number ten and its multiples to represent the idea of completeness. When we see some form of the number ten in the Revelation, God wants us to realize that what is happening and will happen in that given vision is a complete picture of what we can expect to see in the world around us until Jesus returns.*

CHAPTER THREE
The Most Essential Skill for the Revelation

Reading the Pictures

There is one more skill we need to acquire. It may be the most important skill of all if we are going to discern the messages in the pictures God has drawn. That is the skill we employ when we look at any picture or painting and attempt to understand the message of the artist. Some Bible students approach the Revelation like they would approach any other book. Using "book reading skills" they try to understand the "pictures" John describes in the Revelation. This approach leads to much of the confusion that surrounds the Revelation. We can demonstrate this problem as we examine the first picture God draws at the end of chapter one, the Vision of Christ Among the Lampstands.

John describes nine details in the picture of Christ Among the Lampstands. He tells us this picture contained ... *7 lampstands ... a son of man dressed in a robe reaching down to his feet and with a golden sash around his chest.* *14 ... his hair ...white as snow, and his eyes were like blazing fire.* *15 His feet were like bronze glowing in a furnace, and his voice was like the sound of rushing waters.* *16 In his right hand he held seven stars, and out of his mouth came a sharp double-edged sword. His face was like the sun shining in all its brilliance.* (Rev. 1:13-16 NIV) These details present us with an immediate problem. John describes these details in a long list. As such, all the details appear to have the same value. We are left with questions. Does God want us to assign equal value to every detail in a given vision as we search for his message? Do all the details in the pictures have some deeper hidden meaning? These are important questions. But we must realize that these questions grow out of an assumption, the assumption that we are trying to understand a book. If we were standing in front of a picture hanging on a wall, we would never ask these questions. A picture hanging on a wall contains thousands of details. Yet it is obvious as we look at the picture, that the details of the picture do not all carry the same weight when it comes to understanding the meaning of a picture.

This distinction between learning the message of a book and learning the message of a picture hanging on a wall leads us to the key to understanding the Revelation. It lies in remembering that in the book of Revelation John is describing a series of pictures that God drew. In order to understand the message of each vision, we must approach each description as we would approach a painting. Only by taking this approach can we understand the meaning behind the visions. Perhaps the best way I can demonstrate this is to examine a picture with you.

Look closely at this picture. It is a very familiar composition designed by Eric Enstrom, a photographer who lived in the early 1900's in Bovey, Minnesota. This picture was first created as a photograph in 1918. When the picture became  popular, Enstrom's daughter, Rhoda Nyberg of Coleraine, Minnesota, reproduced the photograph as an oil painting. Today most of us have seen one form or another of this painting.

Eric Enstrom gave this picture a "one-word name." You don't have to be an art history expert to know what he called this picture. All you need to do is examine it as you would any painting. The name will be obvious to you. In the painting, we see an old man sitting at a simple wooden table. On the table is a book, a bowl of soup with a spoon, and a loaf of bread with a knife. The man is obviously intending to eat a simple meal. As he does, before he begins, he bows his head, folds his hands, and says …. "Grace." This is the name of the painting. That name conveys the life truth the artist wants us to see. We live in the care of the Lord each day and it is that Lord who provides us with every blessing, including the blessing of food on our table. How fitting that we remember the daily care of God by giving thanks at our tables, saying "grace" if you will.

But here is the point. The only way we can understand the message in the picture is by looking at the whole picture. If we focused our attention on only a small portion of the painting, like the book and the bowl in the lower corner, this approach would lead us further away from  the artist's intended message. For example, we might spend a great deal of time wondering what kind of soup is in the bowl and what the meaning of the soup might be. We might wonder what the book is in the corner and what is the message behind the book. Notice that with each new question we ask as we focus on these details, we move further and further away from the meaning contained in the whole picture. This is the mistake many people make with the pictures in the Revelation. Instead of looking at the whole picture, people focus their attention on the small details of the visions and then try to imagine what these pieces might mean. In the process they lose the intended meaning of the picture itself.

This is what happens with the Vision of Christ Among the Lampstands. Some Bible students employ their active imaginations spending much energy examining the pieces of the vision. They look closely at the *"white hair"* or the *"blazing eyes"* or the *"feet like bronze"* trying to gain deep meaning from these details. They supply well reasoned guesses as to what these images might symbolize. In the end, they lose sight of the main message God intended with the vision. In the Revelation only by examining the whole picture can we gain the message God wants us to learn in any given vision. At times God will help us with this process. He urges us to look at the complete picture in each vision and then God calls our attention to specific details in the vision that reveal the message he wants us to find.

This first vision of Jesus is an excellent example of this. As he explains the meaning of the picture, God highlights the important details in the picture and separates them from the rest. *The mystery of the seven stars that you saw in my right hand and of the seven golden lamp-stands is this: The seven stars are the angels of the seven churches, and the seven lampstands are the seven churches.* (Rev. 1:20 NIV) Of all the details in the picture, God chooses to highlight only two. As Jesus walks among the lampstands, God fixes our attention on the stars and on the lampstands and he tells us that both are metaphors. God says the lampstands *"are the seven churches"* and the stars *"are the angels of the seven churches."* By this emphasis God is explaining that the story of this picture lies in these two details. When we put these two details together with the fact that Jesus is walking among them, we have the story God is telling.

Remember what we learned about the timeframe of the Revelation? Every vision pictures the time between the first coming of Jesus and the second coming of Jesus, and each vision reveals something that will be true for that entire period of time. In this case God is telling us that for the entire New Testament era, Jesus is going to be *"walking among the lampstands."* In Matthew chapter twenty-eight when Jesus ascended into heaven, he spoke the words of the Great Commission to his New Testament Church. *"Go and make disciples of all nations ..."* Jesus finished that command with a promise. The Lord assured us that as we carried his light into this world *"... I will be with you always, to the very end of the age."* The Vision of Christ Among the Lampstands is a picture of this truth. God is revealing that sharing his light in this dark world will occupy his full attention each day. God is promising that Jesus is always going to walk with his churches as they carry out this light-sharing work. During this time God is going to give special care to the pastors of his churches, holding them in his hand and protecting them from harm. This is the story of purpose that God reveals in this first vision.

This is an example of how we must learn to handle the details in the Revelation. The Revelation is a book of pictures. Remember, every picture we see contains many details large and small. In a given painting, the details are not all valued the same. Some carry the meaning of the picture while others merely serve as background. As we approach each new vision in the Revelation, even though the description will list many details of the picture, we must remember to always look at the whole picture to learn what God is teaching. Do not let the individual details of any given picture distract you from the full truth God is revealing in the full picture. Never walk away from examining one of God's visions without gaining a clear understanding of the main message God is conveying. At the same time, we will trust God to lead us to focus our attention on any details in the picture which carry the meaning he wants us to learn.

Chapter Summary

The Revelation is a book of pictures! To read Revelation successfully and to understand the messages God has recorded within this book, we must remember that Revelation is a book of pictures. We must employ the skills we use when studying a picture on a wall if we are going to learn what God is teaching. Some things to keep in mind as we follow this approach:

Always look at the whole picture to learn the message God is revealing. *Do not let yourself get distracted by the smaller details within the picture. Many times these small details within a given picture will deepen our appreciation of what God is saying. However, we must never let these details obscure our ability to see the main message which God is conveying in the vision he created.*

Let God guide you to the meaning he intends you to find in the picture. *God will at times offer guidance in the pictures he presents by highlighting the specific details which carry the meaning he wants us to find. Conversely, when God chooses not to explain a given detail or to supply a meaning for it either in the vision or in the rest of the Bible, the silence of God can be a message telling us that this detail does not carry the meaning of the full picture.*

Let God interpret the meaning of the pictures. *In the Revelation God often uses visions he has previously used in other parts of the Bible. Make sure you consult the other occurrences of a given vision. Often God will, in those instances, explain the meaning he wants us to find in the vision.*

CHAPTER FOUR
The Vision of Christ Among the Lampstands

Revelation Chapter One

We now are ready to read the Revelation. We begin with the first picture which God records in Revelation chapter one. This chapter divides into two parts. The first eight verses form an introduction to the Revelation. In these verses God states his reason for writing this book and he notes the importance this book has for us.

Author's Note: *Make sure you read each section of the Revelation before you read the explanation for that segment recorded in this book. The purpose of this book is to help you gain an understanding of the book of Revelation. You will not be able to achieve that goal unless you make sure you read what God said first. Begin that process now and follow it throughout your study and you will gain a clear understanding of the Revelation. This knowledge will change your life.*

Read Revelation 1:1-3

THE PURPOSE OF THE REVELATION

In his opening words, God reveals his intention in giving us these visions. He wants to *"show his servants what must soon take place."* God is going to show us the future. God will explain what is happening now in the world around us and he will reveal what is going to happen until Jesus comes again. Armed with what we learn, we will understand the events we see each day and at the same time we will be equipped to face the future. God makes it plain that there is an urgency to this message. We dare not put off learning what the Revelation teaches. As God reminds us, *"the time is near."* This is the main point God wants us to understand as we begin our study. What we learn here is essential for living each day.

Once we have that main point clearly in mind, we can take the time to notice some of the lesser points the words of these first three verses reveal. God wants us to see that this is *"the revelation of Jesus Christ."* John wrote the words on the page, but God is the one who gave John the words. John is recording the words and visions Jesus revealed to him.

Some Christians struggle with the next phrase. John tells us that Jesus reveals that *"which God gave him."* Jesus Christ is true God. The Bible clearly says this. As God, Jesus knows all things, the past and the future. He does not need to be "given" such knowledge. Yet we are told that God *"gave"* Jesus this message. We have to remember that the Bible also tells us Jesus is a true human being. As a human being Jesus did not know all things or have all power. As a human being Jesus had to be "given" these things by God. In effect the God in Jesus shared with the man in Jesus godly power. We call this the communication of attributes in theological terms. As a result the Bible sometimes speaks of Jesus from his human perspective. That is what is happening with this phrase.

The last thing we must make sure to notice in these first three verses is the promise God makes regarding our study of the Revelation. God tells us, *"Blessed are those who read and blessed are those who hear and take it to heart."* In the Greek language, the word for "blessed" literally means "happy." God is telling us that those who learn the lessons of the Revelation will be equipped to live lives that are happy and successful. The Revelation equips us to do that and this is God's plan for us.

There is nothing in our lives more important or more immediate than our need to know and to understand what God is teaching in the visions of Revelation. God has much for us to learn and his teachings will change our lives.

Read Revelation 1:4-6

THE GREETING

John identifies himself as the one who is recording these words from God. As we said before, the *"John"* who is writing these words is John the apostle of Jesus, one of the original twelve apostles. He stands at the end of his life having lived to be almost 100 years old. John is writing to *"the seven churches in the province of Asia."* This is our first encounter with the number seven in the Revelation. In this case God applies this number to seven individual congregations that existed during the time of John in Asia Minor, which is part of modern day Turkey. It is clear that John was acquainted with them and perhaps even served them in some capacity.

However, the fact that God uses the number seven here is no accident and carries a meaning we need to notice. Seven in the Revelation carries the message and reminder of the Gospel Covenant. When God uses the number seven, he wants us to remember the Gospel work he is carrying out each day in this world. God is reaching out to all people with the message of salvation through faith in Jesus before it is too late. In this case, God attaches the number seven to his visible church on earth so that we will understand that God is using the visible Christian Church to accomplish his light-sharing task and to fulfill his Gospel Covenant.

Continuing with the greeting, God offers a message of *"grace and peace"* to the people who read the Revelation. Notice this expectation and intention is the opposite of the reaction of many people in our world who read the Revelation. Instead of "peace," many people are terrified by the visions that they see within the book. All they see are the judgments of God warning of terrible things to come. This reaction is no accident. God is sending a message of warning to unbelievers with these images. However, God does not want his believing children to have this reaction to these pictures. It is God's intention that you and I will find comfort and joy as we read his promises in the Revelation. The visions of the Revelation reveal God's promises to his people, promises of peace and safety, promises that assure them that God is with them in this world, that he walks by their side, and that all is well. The Revelation is a message of *"grace and peace"* for God's people even as it is a book announcing judgment to all who oppose God. As we read the Revelation our purpose will be to seek that peace.

God wants us to be very aware that he and he alone is the one writing these words. God reveals himself in this vision with three clear statements. The one speaking is the Father *"who is and who was and who is to come."* God is reminding us of his eternal nature. He is the God who always existed, who alone exists now, and who will always exist. He is the God who identified himself to Moses at the burning bush as the *"I am,"* the God who exists in a world filled with false gods that do not exist.

Next God identifies himself as *"the seven spirits"* before the throne of God. This is a reference to the Holy Spirit, the third person of the Trinity. For the second time in the Revelation, God holds the number seven before our eyes, the number that reminds us of God's Gospel Covenant. In this case God is calling our attention to the role the Holy Spirit plays in the work of establishing God's covenant with each believer. It is the Holy Spirit who creates our connection with the covenant by creating faith in Jesus in our hearts. God confirms this truth in the book of 1 Corinthians. ... *no one can say, "Jesus is Lord," except by the Holy Spirit.* (1 Cor. 12:3b NIV)

Finally God refers to himself as Jesus Christ, and God uses three terms here to describe the second person of the Trinity. Jesus Christ is the *"faithful witness,"* the one who came to this earth to reveal the loving heart God has for sinful mankind. Jesus is also the one who conquered death by rising from the dead on Easter Sunday. Jesus' resurrection is a promise from God that all who believe in him will rise to life on the last day when Jesus comes again. This makes Jesus the *"firstborn from the dead,"* the first one to rise who anticipates the full resurrection of the family of God. With the third term God describes his son as the *"ruler of the kings of the earth."* Jesus is *"King of kings and Lord of lords."* He rules the world right now and nothing happens in this world without his permission. This truth is essential if we are going to understand the visions of the Revelation. God is in full control of all that is happening and he makes all things fit his plan.

God makes one more important point in this greeting which is critical for us to keep in mind. God wants us to remember that he loves us. He is completely on our side and wants to fill our lives with his blessings. God states two proofs of that love. First he *"freed us from our sins"* by sacrificing Jesus in our place. Then he *"made us a kingdom and priests"* in his eyes, treasures who are welcomed in his presence every day. Because of what Jesus did for us, God now sees us as kings and priests.

This is very important to keep in mind as we study the predictions God makes for the world in which we live. The consequences the world faces for living in a broken covenant with him are severe. Even as we read of those consequences and the terrible effect they have on mankind, God wants us to remember that he loves us, his children, and he will keep us safe from these things. Secure in God's love we know that all is well with us no matter what is happening in the world around us.

Read Revelation 1:7,8

THE WARNING!

Verses seven and eight in Revelation chapter one bring us an ominous warning from God. The Revelation contains a message so vital and essential for living in this world, that learning what this book teaches is the most important thing we can do at this moment in our lives. God tells us why this message is so urgent. The world we live in is temporary. Soon Jesus will return and when he does, the world will come to an end. *Look, he is coming with the clouds, and every eye will see him, even those who pierced him; and all the peoples of the earth will mourn because of him. So shall it be! Amen.* (Rev. 1:7 NIV) The end is coming and we need to be ready. That day will not be like Jesus' first coming in a lowly manger in Bethlehem so long ago. This time Jesus will come *"with the clouds,"* visible to all, and *"every eye will see him."* God is not describing a "man-made" event with these words. The second coming of Jesus is a supernatural event. God decides when it will be and all people will know it is from the hand of God when it occurs.

"He is coming with the clouds." This is a warning that affects every day we live, shaping our actions and words by the approaching shadow of the Lord's return. If at any moment the Lord will again appear, we want to make sure we are "living ready" for that event. We want to make sure we are using our lives for the purpose God intended, serving him rather than serving ourselves, living to be a blessing to others as we have opportunity out of love for God. This is who we are -- God's believing children looking forward to his return every day.

Unfortunately, not everyone will heed the warning of the Lord. The fact is many in this world live in opposition to the covenant of faith in Jesus Christ. Theirs is a life defined by a "broken covenant" with the God who made them. For these people the day of the Lord's return will be a time to account to the Lord for their rebellion. God alludes to this with the news that *"all people will mourn because of him."* On the last day when Jesus returns all who lived in the "broken covenant" will see the error of their ways and be filled with regret when they see that it is too late. Their chance for redemption has passed them by. Despair will fill their hearts. Trapped by the chains of selfishness, they wasted the days God gave them by serving themselves when God created them to serve him. Now they face an eternity answering for this terrible choice.

God wants to make sure we understand that this warning comes to us directly from him. God reminds us here that he is the one speaking these words, the *"Alpha and the Omega,"* the author of all life. He is the one from whom all life originates and he is the one to whom all life must answer. The *"Alpha and Omega"* is speaking his warning to us. Let this warning be the caution that informs every word and action of our lives as we anticipate his return.

Read Revelation 1:9-16

THE VISION OF CHRIST AMONG THE LAMPSTANDS

As verse nine begins, we encounter the first picture God drew to equip us for life in this world. The vision God reveals here, of Christ Among the Lampstands, contains the first and most important truth we need to know about this world if we are going to live successfully. John describes the picture for us. As the scene begins, John notes that he was a *"companion in the suffering"* that Christians faced in the persecution of that time. It was 96 AD. It was the time of Emperor Domitian, and Christians throughout the Roman Empire were suffering from persecution. John tells us that he also faced persecution. Evidence of that was that he writes from the island of Patmos where he was in exile. The Roman government had placed John on that island because of *"the testimony of Jesus Christ."* In other words, John was being punished because he dared to tell the story of Jesus.

Patmos is a small island, about 24 square miles. It is located in the

Aegean Sea about 40 miles from the coast of Asia Minor. John tells us about the day he received the Revelation from Jesus. It was the Lord's day, Sunday. John was *"in the spirit."* He was worshiping the Lord and was in meditation at that moment. Suddenly, he heard a loud voice behind him commanding him to write a letter to the seven churches of Asia Minor. John goes on to tell the story. *I turned around to see the voice that was speaking to me. And when I turned I saw seven golden lampstands, [13] and among the lampstands was someone "like a son of man," dressed in a robe reaching down to his feet and with a golden sash around his chest.* (Rev. 1:12,13 NIV) John sees an amazing vision. He sees seven golden lampstands all brightly burning. And walking among those lampstands was none other than Jesus Christ, the risen Savior. *His head and hair were white like wool, as white as snow, and his eyes were like blazing fire. [15] His feet were like bronze glowing in a furnace, and his voice was like the sound of rushing waters. [16] In his right hand he held seven stars, and out of his mouth came a sharp double-edged sword. His face was like the sun shining in all its brilliance.* (Rev. 1:14,15 NIV)

We will find that God often roots the visions of the Revelation in the rich imagery of the Old Testament. This is intentional. God does this to demonstrate the connection between the future events he is revealing and the ancient plan he has been carrying out since the dawn of time. Founding the visions of the Revelation on ancient Old Testament imagery makes it clear that God is completing plans he made from the beginning. This first vision of the Revelation is a strong example of a picture rooted in other Bible pictures.

John describes Jesus with *"white hair"* and *"blazing eyes."* This image reminds us of the description in Daniel chapter seven of the almighty God on his throne on the last day. *As I looked, thrones were set in place, and the Ancient of Days took his seat. His clothing was as white as snow; the hair of his head was white like wool. His throne was flaming with fire, and its wheels were all ablaze.* (Daniel 7:9 NIV) With these details God is picturing the power of the Lord who walks among the lampstands.

What catches our eye as being out of place is the description of a *"sharp doubled-edged sword"* coming out of his mouth. The Lord who walks among the lampstands is armed and his weapon is a sword with two sharp edges. Here we remember what God writes in the book of Hebrews as he describes his holy word. *For the word of God is living and active. Sharper than any double-edged sword, it penetrates even to dividing soul and spirit, joints and marrow; it judges the thoughts and attitudes of the heart.* (Hebrews 4:12 NIV) No doubt John's picture of Jesus here recalls that sharp sword of the Law of God which cuts through our human pride to condemn the sin in our hearts. At the same time the picture reminds us of the sword of the Gospel which cuts through the guilt we carry assuring us of God's love in Christ.

Seeing the connections with other images in the Bible deepens our understanding of the picture God is drawing. However, even as we note the connections to other images in the Bible, we must be careful not to divert our attention from the main message the vision contains. God draws this picture to teach us the first important truth we need to know if we are going to understand this world and be equipped to live in it. God is going to reveal his purpose for allowing this evil world to continue from one day to the next. At the same time God will show us our purpose in life, the reason he grants us another day of life on this earth. God explains all this in the final verses of chapter one.

Read Revelation 1:17-20

THE MYSTERY OF THE SEVEN STARS AND THE SEVEN LAMPSTANDS

God intends that the visions in the Revelation will provide us with truths that will help us understand what is happening in the world every day. At the same time these truths will equip us with the information we need to live successfully and to fulfill God's purpose. John plays an important role in this process. God chose him to reveal the message to us. In these last verses of chapter one God directs John's attention to the task at hand. John tells us of his reaction when he stood before the holy Son of God. John was overwhelmed. *When I saw him, I fell at his feet as though dead.* (Rev. 1:17a NIV) John was stunned by the holiness of the Lord. He was overcome by the sudden clarity of his own guilt and the shame of his own sinfulness. Throughout the Bible this is the universal reaction of sinful people who found themselves standing in the presence of the holy God. Paralyzing fear filled John's heart. He was not worthy to stand before God and so he collapses, falling to the ground as though dead.

The Lord responded with compassion. He placed his right hand on John's shoulder and told him to put his fear aside. *Then he placed his right hand on me and said: "Do not be afraid. I am the First and the Last. ¹⁸ I am the Living One; I was dead, and behold I am alive for ever and ever! And I hold the keys of death and Hades."* (Rev. 1:17b-18 NIV) There is no longer reason for the sinner to cower in fear. The death the sinner deserves has been overcome. Jesus, the *"living one,"* rose from the dead and has conquered it. Now he holds the keys to death in his hand and offers release from death and its fear to all mankind.

The Lord then directs John's attention to the work he has for John to do. *Write, therefore, what you have seen, what is now and what will take place later.* (Rev. 1:19 NIV) God wants to reveal his plan. He wants to show his children what is going to happen in this world until Jesus comes again. He wants us to understand what our eyes will see and our ears will hear. God wants us to be able to look past the chaos in this world to see his plan beneath the surface. John is the one who will write down what we need to know.

The Vision of Christ Among the Lampstands contains the first essential truth all Christians must know. God calls it the *"mystery of the* seven stars and the seven golden lampstands." In the final verse of the chapter, God guides us to what he wants us to learn by pointing to the details of the picture that carry the meaning. This is the pattern God will follow with the visions in the Revelation. Therefore we will not have to guess at the meaning of each vision. When there is something to learn, God will explain that lesson. When God does not supply a meaning for a given item or detail in a vision, we will assume that the item is not central to the lesson God is teaching.

In this vision, as Jesus stands in the midst of the picture, God tells us that there are two details that carry the meaning. *The mystery of the seven stars that you saw in my right hand and of the seven golden lampstands is this: The seven stars are the angels of the seven churches, and the seven lampstands are the seven churches.* (Rev. 1:20 NIV) The stars represent the pastors of the seven churches and the lampstands represent the seven churches.

As you combine what God says with the fact that Jesus walks among them, focus your attention on the lampstands. Therein lies the first thing God wants us to know. There is so much in this world that is ugly and hateful and evil. Every day new horrible things happen, things so terrible that we wonder why God would not simply put an end to this world right now. God answers that question here. Simply put, God tells us, *"It's about the light."* God is showing us his purpose in allowing the world to continue from one day to another, even when he knows horrible things will happen. With each new day God is reaching out to all people with the light of salvation through faith in Christ, before it is too late. He is shining his light into this world through his lampstands. When God has reached everyone he can reach, the world will come to an end. *And this gospel of the kingdom will be preached in the whole world as a testimony to all nations, and then the end will come.* (Matt. 24:14 NIV)

In this case the seven churches represent all the visible Christian churches throughout the full New Testament. Until Jesus returns, he will be shining his light through his churches and their work. He will not leave them alone to do this. For the entire period of time Jesus will walk among them and support them in the important work of sharing that light. The presence of Jesus among the lampstands underscores the importance of this work. God rules the universe and controls all that happens. Yet of all the things that occur, the thing most important to God is the work of the lampstands. It is the only thing that matters. God gives this work his full attention every day. He walks among the lampstands and oversees their work. In effect God is showing us a picture of the "great commission" which he states in Matthew 28. As Jesus ascended into heaven he commanded his church to *"make disciples of all nations"* and he promised *"I am with you always, even to the end of the age."*

As we gaze at this picture which reveals the important work God is doing each day, we find a clear purpose for our lives as well. It is no accident that God gives us another day to live on this earth. Each new day provides us with opportunities to share the light of Jesus and the hope it gives us with as many people as we can in whatever way God allows. Think of how many lives you touch on an average day. Some of the touches are brief and insignificant as we stand in line at the post office or as we interact with the checkout person to pay for our groceries. Some of the touches are more involved as we deal with the people at our place of school or work, or as we embrace the loved ones in our lives. Every touch, whether large or small, is an opportunity to shine our light. By the way we react to shared events and by the way we treat those around us, we can display the hope and confidence God has given us. When we remember that many people in our lives live in darkness and do not know or share in that hope or confidence, we have a chance to shine God's light into their darkness with every touch. Even as the church is a lampstand, each Christian in the church is a lampstand as well. We play a direct role in God's plan and purpose each day.

In this vision we find the first and most important truth we need to learn about our world. As we survey the world around us and note the new acts of evil and violence and loss, it appears as if the world is in chaos. Our senses can detect no pattern or plan for the apparently random atrocities that so frequently occur. God paints the Vision of Christ Among the Lampstands to show us that there is a clear plan and a clear pattern in this world. Through his churches and through his Christians, God is carrying out important work each day, sharing his light with as many as possible, and time is running out.

There is only one important question to ask. *"How far did the light spread today?"* There will come a day when time runs out and the Lord will appear on his throne. Then all will give an account to the Lord for the life with which he entrusted them. This is the defining truth that determines each new day. This is the first thing we must know about this world if we are going to be equipped to live in it and fulfill the purpose God intends for us. This is the first essential truth of the Revelation.

Chapter Summary

The First Essential Revelation Truth

The only reason God allows this world to continue to exist is that he is reaching out to all people in this world with his light, before it is too late! When God has completed that task, the world will come to an end.

The vision reveals God's purpose in allowing this world to exist from one day to the next. *Focusing on the imagery of the "lampstands" and their purpose, God is revealing the first and most important truth we need to know if we are going to understand what is happening in this world. God is using his "light" (the message of the Gospel which tells of salvation for all through faith in Jesus) to reach out to people, before it is too late. On the day that work is completed, the world will come to an end.*

The vision also reveals our purpose as God grants us another day to live. *Each Christian is an individual "lampstand" for the Lord. God gives us new days to live so that we can touch the lives of other people with the hope God has given us through faith in Jesus. This is the purpose of our lives and it represents the most important thing we have to do each day.*

> **Matthew 28:19,20** *Therefore go and make disciples of all nations, baptizing them in the name of the Father and of the Son and of the Holy Spirit, [20] and teaching them to obey everything I have commanded you. And surely I am with you always, to the very end of the age.* (NIV)

> **Matthew 24:14** *And this gospel of the kingdom will be preached in the whole world as a testimony to all nations,*

and then the end will come. (NIV)

Matthew 5:14-16 *You are the light of the world. A city on a hill cannot be hidden.* *[15] Neither do people light a lamp and put it under a bowl. Instead they put it on its stand, and it gives light to everyone in the house.* *[16] In the same way, let your light shine before men, that they may see your good deeds and praise your Father in heaven.* (NIV)

CHAPTER FIVE
The Vision of the
Seven Letters, Part One

Revelation Chapter Two

The Vision of Christ Among the Lampstands showed us the first important truth we need to know about this world. God is sharing his message of light through faith in Jesus with all people before it is too late. This is the message of light which shines each day from God's lampstands. That same vision showed us that each of us is connected to God's purpose. We are individual lampstands, and each day we have new chances to touch the people around us with the hope and confidence God gave us through faith in Jesus. Individually and collectively as God's church, believers are the lampstands of the Lord. While we function as God's lampstands, Jesus walks by our side every step of the way and keeps us safe.

Now God turns his attention to the question of "lampstand expectations." What will it be like to carry God's light into a world filled with darkness, a world that so desperately needs that light? That is the subject of the Vision of the Seven Letters which we find recorded in Revelation chapters two and three. God gives us this vision to prepare us for the task of sharing his light with a world filled with darkness. It will shape our expectations so we will be prepared for what we are going to experience as God's lampstands.

The Vision of the Seven Letters records letters written by God to the seven congregations in Asia Minor. These were seven actual congregations which existed at the time of John. Since they seemed to know the apostle, it is likely that John in the past had served them in some way. We should note that while these are individual letters written to individual congregations that existed at the time of John, taken together, these letters also form a vision or painting that carries the next important message from God. These seven letters form a "collage" of seven panels, with each panel offering a different view of the same message. God is addressing the question of "lampstand expectations." With each new panel God is revealing a different facet of the experience Christians, and the churches they form, will have as they share God's light with this world.

As God's lampstands we have a light which the world desperately needs. This fact might lead us to expect that the world would value the message we bring and would welcome us with open arms. After all, if we stood with many other people in a pitch black room, and we alone possessed a flashlight, we would be very popular and very welcomed. God shows us in the Vision of the Seven Letters that just the opposite will be true in this world. It is a fact that the dark world needs God's light more than anything else. But it is also a fact that the world loves the darkness and hates the light. *This is the verdict: Light has come into the world, but men loved darkness instead of light because their deeds were evil.* (John 3:19-21 NIV) For this reason the world will object to the light and persecute those who bring it. The Vision of the Seven Letters prepares us to expect that experience.

The letters follow a specific structure. Each letter has seven individual parts. The letters begin with the command of God to write to the individual church. God continues the letter by giving the church a description of himself. Usually that description has something to do with the experience of the given congregation, either positive or negative. God follows that description with a commendation. In this case, only the church in Laodicea did not receive a commendation. The commendation is usually followed by a criticism as God notes some area where the darkness of the world has infiltrated the light or the work of the church. The only churches that did not receive any critical comments were Smyrna and Philadelphia. God follows the criticism with an admonition, directing the congregation to face the challenges head on. The letters end with a call to hear what God is saying and to listen to it, followed by a promise to those who hear and who walk God's path.

It is important to note that there are seven churches and seven letters. This number seven is no accident. God uses the number seven in the Revelation to represent his *"Gospel Covenant."* In this case, God reveals seven different examples of how the darkness in this world will hinder or harm those who bear his light. Each of the seven churches is unique and each church has its own unique experience as it shines its light into the world. Some lived in constant challenge from the dark world. Some found the darkness even invaded their church. Some found growth while others found only suffering. However, taken together, the seven letters teach us what to expect as we shine God's light into this dark world. This vision forms a "collage" comprised of seven panels. Not every Christian church or every Christian will experience every one of these conditions. But we will see examples of every one of these pictures in the churches and in the Christians we know. All who carry the light of God will be damaged or afflicted by the darkness around them. By using the number seven, God is assuring us that even though the darkness will cause damage in his churches and to his Christians, God still will use these damaged lampstands to share his light. God knows his churches and his Christians will be flawed because of the opposition of the darkness. He knows they will at times fail to shine the light when they should. Yet God tells us there are "seven" churches. God is assuring us that even though he has chosen imperfect instruments to share his light in the world, he will succeed in shining his light through them. The number "seven" assures us of this.

The Vision of the Seven Letters reshapes our expectations about light-sharing in this world. We might expect that the people of the world would welcome God's message of light and hope and would embrace those who bring that light. The Vision of the Seven Letters tells us otherwise. Darkness hates light. That was true when Jesus came and that will be true for those who follow Jesus. The darkness will oppose the lampstands. The Vision of the Seven Letters prepares us to anticipate this opposition.

Read Revelation 2:1-7

THE LETTER TO EPHESUS

The Vision of the Seven Letters begins with the letter to the church at Ephesus. This first panel in the collage carries the message of God, warning us about one of the dangers of being a lampstand in a world that loves darkness. The congregation at Ephesus was formed by the Apostle Paul on his third missionary journey. Paul spent three years in this city and the resulting congregation may have been the strongest church in the first century. By the time John wrote this letter, the church at Ephesus was almost fifty years old.

From the start Jesus makes it clear that he walks among the Christians at Ephesus and oversees the work they are doing. He expresses pleasure with them, noting how strongly they stand opposed to false teachers. This was a church standing firmly against the darkness. Jesus commends the Ephesians for standing firm and not growing weary in their opposition. *I know your deeds, your hard work and your perseverance. I know that you cannot tolerate wicked men, that you have tested those who claim to be apostles but are not, and have found them false.* [3] *You have persevered and have endured hardships for my name, and have not grown weary.* (Rev. 2:2,3 NIV)

Then Jesus admonished the people of the church. *Yet I hold this against you: You have forsaken your first love.* (Rev. 2:4 NIV) God draws this picture to warn us against the danger that lies within opposing evil. Standing opposed to evil and false teaching is a good thing, something Christians and churches must always do in this dark world. The church at Ephesus did this with much energy. However, there is a danger that we can spend so much energy opposing what we are against, that we forget to make it clear what we are for. The fact is, opposing the darkness of evil is not the same thing as offering the light of God. The people at Ephesus stood so stridently opposed to false teaching and darkness that they failed to offer people light and hope through faith in Jesus. This is what God calls *"forsaking your first love."*

To make sure that the Christians in Ephesus did not misunderstand what God was saying, Jesus includes one more thought. He noted, *But you have this in your favor: You hate the practices of the Nicolaitans, which I also hate.* (Rev. 2:6 NIV) God did not want them to think that he was criticizing them for opposing evil and darkness. God wants his people to oppose the darkness, always. However, God also wants us to always be places of light where people can come and find the hope that God offers through what Jesus has done.

If a church makes this error by forsaking their first love, that church is in great danger. Jesus indicates that with his warning. *Repent and do the things you did at first. If you do not repent, I will come to you and remove your lampstand from its place.* (Rev. 2:5 NIV) You can't be the lampstand of the Lord if you stop offering light to the dark world. Such lampstands are no longer sources of God's light. They become the darkness they oppose and the Lord must remove them from their place.

To those who listen, Jesus promises special reward. *To him who over-comes, I will give the right to eat from the tree of life, which is in the paradise of God.* (Rev. 2:7 NIV) Thousands of years before Jesus gave this promise, God used an angel with a flaming sword to prevent Adam and Eve or any of those who came after them from eating of the tree of life. Now God promises those who share his hope with the dark world that one day they will eat from this tree in heaven forever.

Until Jesus comes again, we will see churches and individual

Christians who fall prey to this error of forsaking their first love, and we will face the same danger ourselves. When this happens, the church or the Christian will begin to define itself by what it opposes. In the eyes of the world they become churches which stand against that which is wrong, but no one knows what they favor or support or offer. In such a church a homosexual, for example, will hear a clear condemnation of the darkness that fills his heart and his life. But that same lost soul will not hear of the hope for him and the forgiveness and strength he can find in the shadow of the cross of Christ. In the end such congregations are so caught up in the fight with darkness that they stop celebrating the light. They assume that by opposing darkness they are offering light. They do not notice that their light has disappeared.

The Ephesian church letter reveals one of the attacks the devil will use against the light until Jesus returns. The devil will attempt to blot out the light by encouraging churches to concentrate so much on opposing darkness, they forget to offer light and hope. The danger is that some Christians will fall into a pattern of thinking that opposing the darkness is shining the light, as if these two actions are one in the same. They will become people who display a strong talent for judging others. All the while they will fail to notice that no one can find hope and forgiveness in the message they offer. As we read the letter to Ephesus, God makes it clear that a church must do the one without forgetting to do the other. Beware the danger of *"forsaking your first love!"*

Read Revelation 2:8-11

The Letter to the Church At Smyrna

With the letter to Smyrna, God shows us that some churches will faithfully offer the light but will face continual rejection. With this new picture God helps us to reshape our view of what constitutes "success" for the work of a lampstand. On the surface in this world, success seems easy to define. Whether you are talking about grocery stores or movie theaters or churches, the world says that success is always about acceptance and growth. So we might expect that the church that gains the praise of the world and experiences growth in numbers would be a successful church. Conversely, a church that does not grow or a church that is rejected by the world would be a failure. Most of us would agree with this way of measuring success. God shows us with his letter to Smyrna that success in God's kingdom of light is much different from success in this world.

Smyrna was an ancient city located at a central and strategic point on the Aegean coast of Anatolia. The ancient city is located at two sites today within modern Izmir, Turkey. Most of the present-day remains date from the Roman era, the majority from after a 2nd century AD earthquake. Today Izmir has 350,000 inhabitants.

The Bible gives us no information about how or when the church in Smyrna was formed. Anecdotal historical information mentions a large Jewish population that inhabited the city in the Roman era. The best assumption is that the Christian congregation in Smyrna grew out of that Jewish population and, subsequently, that the same Jewish population became the source of the persecution the Christian congregation faced.

The congregation in Smyrna was one of only two congregations out of the seven that received no criticism from God. God was pleased with the Christians at Smyrna and the work they did in his name. Jesus expresses his approval beginning with the first words of his letter. Jesus describes himself as the Lord of life, the *"first and the last."* All life originates from him. He is the one who *"died and came to life again."* Jesus is the one who conquered death. This is the Lord who walks by their side and is in full control, even when their eyes and ears may lead them to question that. In the face of persecution and poverty, they should not feel forgotten. Jesus knows what they are facing. He sees the slander of the enemies who claim to represent him, but are of the devil. He still walks among the lampstands.

This present Lord speaks to the heart of his people as he prepares them for the challenge they are facing. Jesus reminds them that even though they have little of what the world values, they are *"rich"* because they walk each day in the favor of the Lord. That favor does not translate into ease, however. For them the road ahead will be hard. Those who offer God's light in Christ to the world will face a powerful enemy in the devil. *Do not be afraid of what you are about to suffer. I tell you, the devil will put some of you in prison to test you, and you will suffer persecution for ten days. Be faithful, even to the point of death, and I will give you the crown of life.* (Rev. 2:10 NIV)

With this verse we encounter another of the metaphoric numbers of the Revelation, this time in the form of the number ten. God uses this number to present the concept of "completeness." Jesus tells the church at Smyrna that their "complete" future will consist of persecution from Satan. He calls it *"ten days of persecution."* They will not find growth in numbers or acceptance from the world for the message they carry. Constant opposition and rejection will be their future even though the church at Smyrna faithfully offers God's light and hope to the world.

This segment of the collage that is the Vision of the Seven Letters alters the way we measure success for churches in this world. God warned us of the world's opposition to the light. *Dear friends, do not be surprised at the painful trial you are suffering, as though something strange were happening to you.* (1 Peter 4:12 NIV) *Do not be surprised, my brothers, if the world hates you.* (1 John 3:13 NIV) Some congregations will experience continual opposition and hatred from the dark world around them as they share the light of God. These churches and Christians will faithfully present God's light to the world, but they will face continual rejection. God drew the picture of the church at Smyrna to alert us to this truth.

Sometimes in this world God's churches will be rejected. The new truth God reveals in this collage is that churches which experience the world's rejection are not necessarily failing. The world's condemnation does not mean they are "doing it wrong" when it comes to sharing the light God gave them. God tells them in his letter that the persecution these churches face is also part of his plan. They should not be dismayed. All is well. God is pleased with them as they walk this hard road. In the kingdom of God, for these churches, the rejection by the world is a measure of success.

In the face of this constant trial and hardship, God urges the Christians at Smyrna to continue to do the thing that makes them a successful church. God urges them to be *"faithful even to the point of death."* He promises them a *"crown of life"* to wear for eternity in his presence. The Lord goes on to assure them that if they continue to serve him faithfully, they will *"not be hurt at all by the second death."*

The Revelation speaks of the coming threat of the *"second death."* The first death is the one with which we are all familiar, the moment our bodies die on this earth. The second death refers to the events of Judgment Day. When God comes again, he will call all mankind to stand before his throne for judgment. Those who do not believe in Jesus will be condemned to an eternity in hell, separated from God forever. This eternal condemnation is what the Bible calls the *"second death."* There is no escape once that sentence is imposed. There is only an eternity of regret. Jesus points to that event and tells the people of Smyrna to lift up their eyes. They may face hardship now, but they are safe from that terrible moment in the future.

God draws this picture through his letter to the congregation in Smyrna to teach us how to measure success for his church in this dark world. God is teaching us that success in his church is not properly measured by accumulating new members and dollars. Real success in God's kingdom is measured by *"faithfulness"* in sharing his light. We must remember that the lampstands of the Lord are shining their light into a dark world where people love darkness instead of the light. This is a world that lives in constant rebellion against the covenant of God. Not only does the world not accept their light. The world condemns them and persecutes them for shining the light.

The new truth about churches that God reveals in his letter to Smyrna is that we should not be surprised to find faithful churches in this world that do not grow. We should not be surprised to find churches that face continual persecution and condemnation from the world around them. This rejection by the dark world does not mean those congregations are failing God as witnesses. Just the opposite is true. These churches and the Christians in them, like the congregation in Smyrna, are accomplishing exactly what God wants. They are faithfully shining the light of the Lord. They are providing opportunity for those in darkness to hear the truth. Don't measure them by the reception the world gives that light. Measure the success of a church by its faithful commitment to shining God's light in all circumstances. Sometimes the best measure of a congregation's success is found in the strident opposition from the darkness. Some lampstands of the Lord will find only rejection in this world.

Read Revelation 2:12-17

THE LETTER TO PERGAMUM

With the letter to the church at Pergamum, God introduces us to a new truth about the light. That truth is simply this. Light must destroy darkness, or it is not light! This was a truth the people in the church at Pergamum forgot. Mindful of how hard it is to stand opposed to darkness, and wanting to avoid continual rejection like the church at Smyrna faced, the people in the church at Pergamum tried to find an easier road to travel. They decided to compromise with the darkness rather than oppose it.

Their example is important for us to note. We will see Christians and churches in our world make this same mistake repeatedly until Jesus returns. It is yet another example of the damage that we can expect the darkness to cause the light. In these churches you will hear no message condemning the darkness. Such a message would be offensive to the darkness. Instead their message will be accepting, welcoming, positive in every case. When darkness enters their presence, the churches will offer no objection or rebuke at all. The goal will be to make the darkness comfortable. Their hope will be to make friends with the people in darkness in order to win them over. What these churches and these Christians forget is that light cannot tolerate darkness without extinguishing the light. This is the lesson God teaches with this third panel of the collage, the panel for the church at Pergamum. While we will find churches and Christians who compromise with the darkness, the Lord makes it clear that the path of compromise is a path the lampstands of the Lord cannot travel.

The Lord introduces himself as the one who *"has the sharp double-edged sword."* We saw this picture of the Lord in the Vision of Christ Among the Lampstands in Revelation chapter one. There the sword represented the word of the Lord, the weapon through which the Lord will put all things under his feet. The church that dares to stand for the light of the Lord will need to arm itself with the weapon of God's word if it is going to be able to stand against the darkness. There is no other way! Jesus wants this truth to fill the minds of the congregation in Pergamum as he writes to them.

Pergamum was an ancient Greek city located 16 miles from the Aegean Sea. Today you will find remains of this city located north and west of the Turkish city of Bergama. In John's day Pergamum was the political center of the region. History tells us that this ancient city had a very dark spiritual side. Pergamum had three temples dedicated to the worship of the Roman emperor and another temple dedicated to the goddess Diana. With the strong presence of idol worship, it is no surprise that Jesus describes this city as a place where *"Satan had his throne."*

The darkness brought persecution on this congregation and they had suffered loss as a result. A man named Antipas, most likely a member of their congregation, was martyred in this darkness. To their credit, in the face of persecution and opposition, the followers of the Lord did not turn away from him. Jesus takes note of that truth by commending them for remaining *"true to his name"* even during those times of terrible danger.

That said, it is apparent that the Christians in Pergamum had made a dangerous accommodation with the darkness even as they tried to remain faithful to the Lord. We saw the church at Ephesus grow hard and intolerant as they stood against the evil around them. The people of Pergamum took the opposite path. They continued to support the Lord each day in their hearts. But they decided that they did not need to display their support for their Lord or their opposition to the darkness for others to see. That was courting unnecessary danger in their minds. So they compromised with or accommodated the false teachings of Balaam and of the Nicolaitans. *Nevertheless, I have a few things against you: You have people there who hold to the teaching of Balaam, who taught Balak to entice the Israelites to sin by eating food sacrificed to idols and by committing sexual immorality. 15 Likewise you also have those who hold to the teaching of the Nicolaitans.* (Rev. 2:14,15 NIV)

Balaam was the ancient false prophet who was hired by the Moabite king to curse God. When God prevented Balaam from pronouncing a curse on Israel, Balaam earned his wages by teaching the people of Moab to entice Israel into idol worship through promiscuous sexual behavior. In this way Israel incurred the wrath of God and his curse by trying to be both for God and for idols at the same time.

The Christians in Pergamum followed a similar path. They decided it was wiser to tolerate evil and darkness rather than to oppose it. In this way they thought they would make darkness comfortable and win them over to God. By their silent acceptance, the people of this church gave the impression that the darkness was not a problem for them or for God.

This was a church of the Lord which no longer chose to fight the battle for the Lord. Jesus in his admonition shows them this approach was not acceptable in his eyes. *Repent therefore! Otherwise, I will soon come to you and will fight against them with the sword of my mouth.* (Rev. 2:16 NIV) If a church whom Jesus entrusted with the light decides not to oppose the darkness, the light is no longer shining for others to see. Yet this is a battle that will be fought. If a church will not fight against the darkness, Jesus will come and do battle himself. Jesus calls upon this church to repent of its "tolerance."

Jesus concludes this letter with a threefold promise. Reminding them simultaneously of the bread from heaven which Israel ate in the wilderness and the bread of life which Jesus offered the Samaritan woman, Jesus points them to the *"hidden manna."* Jesus promises them a *"white stone,"* perhaps indicating a favorable judgment before God in heaven. He also promises them a *"new name,"* a new identity in the family of God.

Standing for the light is condemnation of the darkness. When you stand for the light, you stand against the darkness. The church at Pergamum tried to avoid this conflict by finding a "middle ground" where they could be for the light but, at the same time, not offend the darkness. This example prepares us to expect to see that same action at times in the Christians and in the churches of God in this world. Under threat from the darkness, seeking favor from the world rather than condemnation, we will encounter churches and Christians in them who seek compromise. They will affirm that in their hearts they stand for the light, but at the same time they will hide that light from the world around them to avoid offending darkness. In such churches, the message that all are welcomed on every path in life no matter how dark, will be presented. They will give the impression that darkness is welcomed and valued here. Christians who follow this path will live each day in relationships with people on the path of darkness and will voice no objection or discomfort. It will appear that the darkness is no problem for them. Darkness will find a home in such places and be comfortable, for it will find no light to disturb it.

Maybe you have seen churches and Christians who travel the path of compromise with the darkness. To all churches and to all Christians who follow the Pergamum path of accommodation and compromise, the Lord says in his letter that the battle is unavoidable. Light must destroy the darkness or it ceases to be light! God calls all such churches to "repent." The battle with darkness must be fought. If God's church will not fight it, then God will come and fight it himself. Hear the warning of the one who holds the doubled-edged sword.

Read Revelation 2:18-28

THE LETTER TO THYATIRA

The fourth panel in the collage of the Vision of Seven Letters draws a picture of the congregation in Thyatira. There we find the example of a church which traveled further down the road of interacting with darkness than the church at Pergamum. The apostle Paul once asked, *For what do righteousness and wickedness have in common? Or what fellowship can light have with darkness?* (2 Cor. 6:14 NIV) On the surface, the answer would seem to be nothing. Light is the opposite of darkness. Surely the two cannot exist together. *Can both fresh water and salt water flow from the same spring?* (James 3:11 NIV) The light of God separates us from the darkness and that change alters the way we live. Darkness no longer fits in our lives. For this reason you might assume it would be impossible to convince a Christian that engaging in works of darkness would somehow be acceptable to God.

Yet this is exactly the attack Satan used at Thyatira, and it is an attack he will continue to use against some in God's churches until Jesus returns. The devil will try to convince us that we can be the light of

God and still walk on the path of darkness with no harm to the light. In fact the devil will make it seem like those Christians who walk in the path of darkness are enhancing their ability to use the light. This was the attack the devil made on the church in Thyatira through a false teacher Jesus calls "Jezebel."

Thyatira was located about 35 miles southeast of Pergamum. It was a very small city, but a busy commercial center. While we know nothing about how the congregation there was formed, we do know that a woman from Thyatira named Lydia was very instrumental in founding the church at Philippi. Some speculate that she may have had a hand in starting the congregation in her home town too. However, the Bible is silent on this matter.

Jesus introduces himself as the *"Son of God."* What he finds among his lampstands in this small congregation offends him. Some think that in its path of engaging in the darkness, the church at Thyatira was one of the churches most corrupted by the darkness. However, Jesus begins with a commendation, noting that there were some within the church that were striving to serve him and to walk in the light. *I know your deeds, your love and faith, your service and perseverance, and that you are now doing more than you did at first.* (Rev. 2:19 NIV) In spite of the attack of darkness, they were still a church possessing the light. Some in the church had faith in the word of God, and they persevered.

But there was a problem in this church. Jesus points it out in his criticism. *Nevertheless, I have this against you: You tolerate that woman Jezebel, who calls herself a prophetess. By her teaching she misleads my servants into sexual immorality and the eating of food sacrificed to idols.* (Rev. 2:20 NIV) The congregation had a woman in their midst who claimed to speak for God. Jesus calls her *"Jezebel"* after the evil queen who introduced the worship of false gods into Israel in the Old Testament. In Thyatira this woman taught that having the light did not mean you had to give up the deeds of darkness. She taught you could be light and walk in darkness at the same time, and still enjoy God's favor. As a result, some began to fill their lives with the immoral actions of the world around them. This made the light look the same as the darkness to the outsider.

Jesus responded to the false teaching of this woman with patience. *I have given her time to repent of her immorality, but she is unwilling.* (Rev. 2:21 NIV) Some might expect that when a false teacher appears in the church, the Lord of heaven would respond with immediate punishment to teach her and all around her a lesson. Instead, the Lord in patience withheld her punishment so that she might have time to repent and turn from this darkness. This is the same patience the Lord shows to all mankind and always has.

In this case the woman wasted her time of grace, and now she and all who follow her were facing the Lord's wrath. *So I will cast her on a bed of suffering, and I will make those who commit adultery with her suffer intensely, unless they repent of her ways. ²³ I will strike her children dead. Then all the churches will know that I am he who searches hearts and minds, and I will repay each of you according to your deeds.* (Rev. 2:22,23 NIV) With the Lord there is no such thing as tolerating evil. Those who walk in darkness will face God's wrath.

Having said this, Jesus now encourages the faithful in Thyatira to continue to walk in his light. *Now I say to the rest of you in Thyatira, to you who do not hold to her teaching and have not learned Satan's so-called deep secrets (I will not impose any other burden on you): ²⁵ Only hold on to what you have until I come.* (Rev. 2:24,25 NIV) Jesus does not define the *"deep secrets"* to which he refers. Some speculate that the false prophetess in Thyatira was teaching that you had to be well acquainted with the path of evil if you were going to know how to oppose it. Therefore those who followed her teachings experimented with the path of darkness so they could be more skilled at defending the light. Those who carry the light of the Lord in their heart recognize this idea as yet another of the lies Satan tells.

Those who remain faithful to the Lord, avoiding this temptation, will find the Lord's reward and blessing. Jesus promises *"authority."* The promise of authority recalls the words of God. *You will rule them with an iron scepter; you will dash them to pieces like pottery.* (Psalm 2:9 NIV) Jesus is the *"King of kings and the Lord of lords."* He is the creator and ruler of the universe. Time and again in the Bible the Lord promises that those who follow him will rule with him for eternity. The authority which Jesus promises here is part of that continuing promise to his followers. The *"morning star"* is a more obscure promise God makes. To see the morning star you must arise while it is still dark. This star burns bright against the dark night sky just before dawn. Some think Jesus is simply relating the promise which Paul looked forward to with such hope, the day when *"we will see him as he is"* in all his glory.

The church in Thyatira presents an important picture of the New Testament church and New Testament Christians. We need to be fully aware of the attack of darkness the devil used at Thyatira, for we will see this attack in our lives and in the churches around us. When the devil cannot make us reject the light, he instead will entice us to keep our hold on the darkness. This *"both light and darkness"* approach has great appeal to the sinful nature within all of us. Darkness looks like fun. Surely engaging in this fun will not change who we are! That is the lie the devil tells. With this lie he causes Christians to engage in acts of darkness while still convincing themselves that their actions do not change their hold on the light.

In the early church the New Testament shows that the devil did great damage to the church with this method of attack. The Apostle Paul in 2 Corinthians, the Apostle Peter in his second letter, the Apostle John in his first letter, and Jude all warn against this error. Each writer notes that Christians had fallen prey trying to be both light and darkness at the same time. The devil will attack us with the lie that darkness and light can exist together. We will see many people deceived by this lie until Jesus returns. Christians will tell themselves that they can remain faithful to the light in their hearts while they engage in the dark actions of the world around them. They will believe they can be part of the darkness without cost to the light. Christians and the church cannot be light while they walk in darkness. Heed the warning of John who summarizes the lesson of Thyatira with these words: *God is light; in him there is no darkness at all. ⁶ If we claim to have fellowship with him yet walk in the darkness, we lie and do not live by the truth.* (1 John 1:5,6 NIV)

Chapter Summary

The Second Essential Revelation Truth

The Darkness will Oppose the Light and the Lampstands who bear it!

God reveals what it will be like to be a Lampstand for the Lord sharing God's light with a world that loves the darkness! *The world trapped in the darkness of the curse of sin and separated from God by that darkness, needs God's "light" more than anything else. Yet the darkness will hate the light! Therefore the world will oppose the light and those who bring that light to them. God reveals this truth in the Vision of the Seven Letters. The vision forms a "collage" of seven panels with each panel depicting a different experience that churches and Christians will have as they offer God's light to the darkness. Not all churches and not all Christians will have all seven experiences pictured in the "collage." However, taken together, this "collage" forms a picture of the complete New Testament experience the lampstands of the Lord can expect to have.*

Note also that God paints "seven" panels. Using that number God wants us to remember, though the darkness opposes and in many cases damages the light and the lampstands, God will still use these flawed vessels to accomplish his important goal of reaching the world with his light before it is too late!

> **John 1:4,5** *In him was life, and that life was the light of men.* *⁵ The light shines in the darkness, but the darkness has not understood it. (NIV)*

> **John 3:19-21** *This is the verdict: Light has come into the world, but men loved darkness instead of light because their deeds were evil. ²⁰ Everyone who does evil hates the light, and will*

not come into the light for fear that his deeds will be exposed. ²¹ But whoever lives by the truth comes into the light, so that it may be seen plainly that what he has done has been done through God. (NIV)

1 John 1:6-7 *If we claim to have fellowship with him yet walk in the darkness, we lie and do not live by the truth. ⁷ But if we walk in the light, as he is in the light, we have fellowship with one another, and the blood of Jesus, his Son, purifies us from all sin. (NIV)*

CHAPTER SIX
The Vision of the Seven Letters, Part Two

Revelation Chapter Three

We are half way through our study of the Vision of the Seven Letters. We find the final three letters in Revelation chapter three. As we begin this final step, it is important to keep our focus on the lesson God wants us to learn here. In the Vision of the Seven Letters, God is showing us what we are going to experience as we carry out the task of sharing his light with the dark world around us. Taken together, the letters form a picture of the full experience God's church will have in a world that hates the light.

The message God is revealing here has two general parts. First God is showing us that the darkness will oppose, hinder, and in some cases, damage the light. God wants us to be prepared for that. At the same time, by using the number seven, God is reminding us that even though the churches and Christians will be damaged by the darkness, God is still going to use them to accomplish his goal of reaching out with his light. Seven reminds us that this work is going on through what we see in the pictures.

Read Revelation 3:1-6

THE LETTER TO THE CHURCH AT SARDIS

The apostle Paul warned us in 2 Corinthians that "...*Satan himself masquerades as an angel of light.*" This we must keep in mind as we read God's letter to the church at Sardis. In this church the devil used a new and more dangerous attack on the light. He taught some in Sardis to take deeds of light and turn them into deeds of darkness, all the while making people think that they were still deeds of light. This was not a new tactic for Satan. In Acts chapter five a man named Ananias and his wife Sapphira followed a similar path. They gave an offering to create an impression to others in the church that they were honoring God with all that they had. Their offering appeared to be an act of light. They wanted people to think that their gift was an act of great devotion to God. In reality it was an attempt to gain the praise of people. Their "light" was actually "darkness."

It is important for us to study this letter because the devil still tempts Christians to follow this path today, turning what are accepted works of light into actual works of darkness. When the devil succeeds in this in a Christian or in a church, the light becomes darkness even as it is celebrated as light. In the church at Smyrna we learned that sometimes what appears to be failure in the church is really success. The church at Sardis will show us the opposite truth. Sometimes what looks like success in the church is really failure.

Sardis was located on the banks of the Pactolus River about 60 miles inland from Ephesus and Smyrna. In ancient times Sardis was one of the most prosperous cities of the ancient world, in part due to the gold deposits found on the shores of the Pactolus River. By the first century and the Christian era, with Sardis under Roman control, the glorious and wealthy aura was long gone.

Jesus introduces himself to this church as the one … *who holds the seven spirits of God and the seven stars.* Jesus had firsthand information about their spiritual condition. He sent the Holy Spirit to them to create faith and he sent pastors to them to tend their faith. Jesus is very concerned for them. *I know your deeds; you have a reputation of being alive, but you are dead. ² Wake up! Strengthen what remains and is about to die, for I have not found your deeds complete in the sight of my God.* (Rev. 3:1,2 NIV) The church at Sardis was a congregation in great danger. They appeared to be alive based on their visible activities. In truth, in God's eyes, their actions were proof that darkness and death were their reality.

The problem was what Jesus calls *"incomplete deeds."* The people in Sardis fell into a pattern of religious behavior and actions which appeared to be pleasing to God. Their actions appeared to say that God mattered to them, but the truth was, in their hearts they served themselves. What appeared to be "spiritual life" in them was, in the eyes of God, clear evidence of darkness and "spiritual death." Jesus gives the warning to wake up before all life disappears from the church. There were still a few in Sardis who were alive in the Lord. The Lord promises those who remain in him will one day be *"dressed in white"* wearing the perfect life of the Lord in heaven and rejoicing that their names are written in the Book of Life.

The temptation the devil used to bring darkness into the church at Sardis is still a method of attack he uses today against Christians and their churches. His goal is to turn recognized acts of light into acts of darkness. We can see this phenomenon in the popular *"self-improvement churches"* of our day. Such churches often attract thousands with their message. Week after week they present messages of self-improvement, offering five easy steps to a better, happier life. These churches prominently display Bibles giving the impression that God himself advocates and offers this advice for successful living. The message is so positive and so hopeful that people do not even notice the focus has changed. The church is encouraging them to serve themselves to find happier lives. Serving God is pushed into the background. All of this is offered in God's name as if it is what God says. In such churches you will not hear anything about the depravity of the human heart or the sinful condition of mankind. You will not hear much talk of the need for a Savior in Jesus Christ. In place of the Gospel you will hear advice about improving the way you live so your life will be joyful and filled with blessings. These churches appear successful and active. Thousands of people flock to them each week. To the world they appear to be places of light, active and alive. In truth, they are places of darkness where people gather to focus on making themselves happier. In them light has become darkness.

We can see the same "Sardis problem" in churches which focus their message and efforts on "improving society" by working to right the world's wrongs. These churches target societal issues like poverty or disease or disaster and they offer people a chance to "make a difference" in this world by making the world a better place. What could be more God-pleasing then working to rid the world of poverty or to help those less fortunate than themselves? Again, to the world around them, these churches appear to be beehives of activity filled with people committed to God. From the outside it looks like they are dedicated to carrying out God's will. The reality is far different. The satisfaction offered in these places comes from feeling that you "made a difference in the world," that you proved you had special value for all to see in the cause you support. Those who join them in these causes are promised the satisfaction of knowing that they have proven their moral worth for all to see by their caring activities. Again, you hear nothing in these churches about sin and the need for a Savior. That light is gone and what you find in its place is darkness that masquerades as light.

Sardis teaches us important "light lessons." When God put faith in our hearts he set us free through that faith from the chains of selfishness into which we were born. Faith sets us free to live our lives for God, free to do his will and to serve him. The devil will use the Sardis temptation to rob us of this freedom. He will offer us chances to serve ourselves while telling us that this is just another way to do God's will. The devil focuses our attention on our actions and then highlights the good we gain from what we do. We hardly even notice he has taken our attention off of serving God because we are so busy improving ourselves. The result is the appearance of life in our actions, as if God is the center of our attention. The truth is we are no longer sharing God's light, and our "light" has turned into "darkness." Jesus warns against this result. *But if your eyes are bad, your whole body will be full of darkness. If then the light within you is darkness, how great is that darkness!* (Matt. 6:23 NIV) Sardis is a warning we must heed. Examine your life each day asking who it is you serve. Make sure that the "light" with which you guide your steps is "light" and not "darkness."

Read Revelation 3:7-13

THE LETTER TO PHILADELPHIA

Sales depend on the salesmen! Right? The better a person is at selling a product, the more the product sells. This is a common truth in our world. Some transfer this truth to the church of God and think that the reception the world gives the light is dependent on the quality of the presentation the light bearer makes.

The letter to the church in Philadelphia will reveal a new truth. In this letter God reveals this simple truth: God is responsible for the growth in his church! Paul said that long before in these words. *I planted the seed, Apollos watered it, but God made it grow. ⁷ So neither he who plants nor he who waters is anything, but only God, who makes things grow.* (1 Corinthians 3:6-8 NIV) The power lies in the word alone. The one who witnesses does not make the word more effective or powerful by the way he delivers the message. Churches and Christians within them shine the light and God produces the results. The church at Philadelphia is a clear example of this truth.

The city of Philadelphia is located about thirty miles southeast of Sardis. Philadelphia in the time of John appears to have been a city of great commercial importance. It was known as the "gateway to the East." Philadelphia was also known in the time of John for its many temples and cultic festival days. The Bible gives us no information as to when or how the church at Philadelphia was formed. We gain the impression from the letter God wrote that the congregation was small in comparison to churches in other communities.

Jesus introduces himself to the church at Philadelphia as the one ... *who holds the key of David. What he opens no one can shut, and what he shuts no one can open.* (Rev. 3:7 NIV) These words recall the fact that Jesus Christ is *"the faithful witness"* who came to this earth to reveal the Father's heart to mankind. This first witness now shows them the path of witnessing which will be theirs to walk. To stress the importance of their work, Jesus announces that he possesses *"the keys of David."* Jesus possesses the keys to God's kingdom. Only he can open the door to heaven and only he can close it.

This truth will be especially important to the Christians in Philadelphia. Jesus explains why in his next words. ... *I know that you have little strength, yet you have kept my word and have not denied my name.* (Rev. 3:8 NIV) The congregation had *"little strength."* We can assume Jesus is commenting on the worldly resources available to them. They had no important people in their church and no connections with the world around them. Most likely they were not people who were rich and powerful and the congregation itself was small in number. A small group like this would be unnoticed by the world. It would also have very little to attract the world to them.

Yet Jesus says, *See, I have placed before you an open door that no one can shut.* (Rev. 3:8 NIV) The term *"open door"* is not a new term in the Bible. Paul talked about God giving him an open door in the city of Corinth, meaning that he had opportunities to preach the Gospel and have people welcome it. In this case the Lord promised this little weak band of Christians that they would have an open door when it comes to presenting his message. People would welcome the message they brought and they would see a harvest from this work, all due to the Lord's power.

Jesus goes on to make two more promises. *I will make those who are of the synagogue of Satan, who claim to be Jews though they are not, but are liars—I will make them come and fall down at your feet and acknowledge that I have loved you.* (Rev. 3:9 NIV) There were enemies among the Jewish population in their city who were slandering their good name and lying about them. Jesus promised one day these enemies would acknowledge for all to see that they were God's people. And God promises that when persecution comes to the rest of Christendom, he would keep them safe from that persecution. *Since you have kept my command to endure patiently, I will also keep you from the hour of trial that is going to come upon the whole world to test those who live on the earth.* (Rev. 3:10 NIV)

With that God makes one final promise to this little church. *Him who overcomes I will make a pillar in the temple of my God. Never again will he leave it. I will write on him the name of my God and the name of the city of my God, the new Jerusalem, which is coming down out of heaven from my God; and I will also write on him my new name.* (Rev. 3:12 NIV) To stand in the presence of God and be accepted by him is the greatest hope a child of God can have. God promises that and a new identity. Not only will the enemies recognize that they belonged to God. All the world will see that by the new name God writes on them.

The lesson of this letter and the truth it reveals is important to remember. It is the lesson the Lord taught in his parable of the sower and the seed. The sower scattered his seed on four different kinds of soil and only one of those types of soil produced a crop. The sower's job was to spread the seed. The rest was up to God. When it comes to sharing what God has done, the message we deliver is not dependent on our choosing the right words or saying them in the right way. The reception of the message is a matter between God and the hearer. Our job is to share the message. God produces the growth.

We already saw that witnessing produces different results in different situations. We noted in Smyrna that sometimes rejection by the world is success in God's church. In Sardis we saw that acceptance by the world appears to be success when it is often failure. Here we see it is the Lord who determines the result. God produces the growth. Our job is to witness to his name, to share his hope with those around us, but we do not produce results.

Too often in this world we will find Christians and churches that forget this truth. Facing rejection from the world as they witness to the light, some will be tempted to "help the light along" by trying to appeal to the world with what the world wants. Some may use their personalities to draw the world to them. Some may edit God's message to make it more world friendly. All of them with the best of intentions are trying to help God along. The problem with such approaches is that they are forgetting the truth God teaches in Philadelphia. Our job is to shine God's light. God alone is responsible for the results that come from shining that light.

This truth also keeps us safe when we as God's lampstands face rejection from the world. We often wonder if the problem is us. Maybe we did not present the light with the "right" words or maybe we would have convinced them if we had taken a different approach. God reminds us in Philadelphia that it is he and he alone who gives an "open door," who causes people to be able to see the light. It is not a matter of saying the right words at the right time in the right way. How we say what God has done does not make the light more successful. The power lies in the Gospel message, not in the presentation. God gives the growth and the same God gives the words. Remember Jesus telling his disciples when they stand before kings not to worry about what to say? *But when they arrest you, do not worry about what to say or how to say it. At that time you will be given what to say, [20] for it will not be you speaking, but the Spirit of your Father speaking through you.* (Matt. 10:19,20 NIV) The Holy Spirit provides the words and governs the reaction. So as you carry the light of God into the world, carry with you the lesson of Philadelphia. Your job is to shine the light. God's job is to cause the growth.

Read Revelation 3:14-22

THE LETTER TO THE CHURCH AT LAODICEA

No one who puts his hand to the plow and looks back is fit for service in the kingdom of God. (Luke 9:62 NIV) Common sense, right? Even for people who never have farmed! We all know that a farmer pulling a plow in his field must keep his eye on where he is going. Straight furrows don't happen by themselves. Plowing takes concentration and full attention. The same is true when walking the path of faith and shining the light of the Lord into the darkness. Christians must keep their full attention on the path and fully commit to the journey. Nothing less will do.

This is exactly the place where the devil will stage yet another attack on the light. The devil uses lies to try and make Christians separate the faith in their hearts from the actions in their lives. The devil tempts Christians to believe that they can have faith in their hearts and not live that faith in their lives. When these lies deceive the Christian, darkness invades his heart and it invades the church. The church at Laodicea, the final panel in the collage that is the Vision of the Seven letters, is an example of that. The letter Jesus writes to them warns against this final danger.

The city of Laodicea was located in the southwest of Phrygia, on the river Lycus, about 10 miles from Colossae. The Bible gives us no direct information on how or when or by whom the Christian congregation was formed in this city. We know that Paul wrote a letter to this city, but we do not have the letter he wrote. Other than in Paul's letter to the Colossians, the only other place the Bible mentions the congregation is here in the Revelation. What we do know is that the congregation did last several hundred years after John received this vision. Historians record that the church had a formal council in Laodicea in 361 AD and that meeting was one of the church-wide meetings at which the canon of Scripture was determined. Today there is not a Christian church in Laodicea.

Jesus identifies himself to these Christians as the one who is *"the faithful and true witness."* This is the Lord who is and always has been fully committed to them and to their salvation. He is the *"Amen,"* the one who affirms that God is committed to saving the world through his Son. This Lord, who never held back from them, has noticed that these Christians cannot make the same claim to him. That is the strong criticism the Lord brings. *I know your deeds, that you are neither cold nor hot. I wish you were either one or the other!* (Rev. 3:15 NIV) These were "half-Christians," people who said they believed in Jesus in their hearts but did not lift a finger to shine his light in their words and actions. It is of this type of Christian that Jesus once said, *He who is not with me is against me, and he who does not gather with me scatters.* (Matt. 12:30 NIV) The light that decides it does not feel like shining is not a light at all. Lights must shine. It is their very nature. The light that does not shine is darkness. Laodicea was filled with this darkness.

For this reason the Lord speaks a strong word of admonition demanding immediate change. *So, because you are lukewarm—neither hot nor cold—I am about to spit you out of my mouth.* (Rev. 3:16 NIV) Full commitment is the only path to serve the Lord. This job cannot be done half-heartedly. The Lord will spit them out of his mouth if they do not change their direction. The Lord goes on to urge them immediately to repent. *You say, 'I am rich; I have acquired wealth and do not need a thing.' But you do not realize that you are wretched, pitiful, poor, blind and naked. 18 I counsel you to buy from me gold refined in the fire, so you can become rich; and white clothes to wear, so you can cover your shameful nakedness; and salve to put on your eyes, so you can see.* (Rev. 3:17,18 NIV) It is time to realize that uncommitted lampstands are not lampstands at all. They may tell themselves they are still of the Lord, that they are rich in his favor, but it is not the truth. It is time to recognize that their selfish path is spiritual poverty. It is time to embrace the salvation the Lord won for them. Even now Jesus was standing at the door, knocking. Even his voice of rebuke is a measure of his love for them. Those who hear will find the reward of a throne in heaven ruling with Jesus and with all who overcome.

The Laodicean Christians found the temptation of darkness lurking within the blessings flowing from the Lord's hand. As God amply provided for these Christians and their needs were met each day, the Christians were distracted from the path of shining their light into the world. They found themselves living their lives separate from the faith God gave them, all the while telling themselves that nothing had changed. On Sunday they spent their "hour" in worship. The rest of the week, they lived to please themselves. This is the path of the "lukewarm Christian."

The lesson of this letter is one that fits in the lives of every child of God. Who has not heard the lie the devil whispers telling us we can have faith without putting that faith into action in our lives? In that lie the "lukewarm Christian" is born. The truth is, apathy is darkness in another form. This darkness plagues Christian churches today. It is common today to see churches with huge "memberships" and empty pews. It is common to see churches today with long lists of members, and yet they struggle to find even a few hands to volunteer for kingdom work. It is common today to find people who will say they are Christians, but their lives and actions and words bear no trace of any commitment to serving the Lord. The apathetic Christian is the expectation today. The committed Christian is rare. The Lord warns us through Laodicea against this lie. *He who is not with me is against me, and he who does not gather with me scatters.* (Matt. 12:30 NIV) Christianity does not have a "lukewarm" option!

The Seven Panels of the Collage:

Ephesus -- *While churches and Christians must strongly oppose darkness, they must never think opposition to darkness is the same thing as offering light. Do not forsake your first love!*

Smyrna -- *Offering God's light faithfully in this dark world will not always produce acceptance and growth. Some churches and Christians will find only rejection and persecution in this world as they faithfully offer God's light. In God's kingdom, faithfulness is the measure of success.*

Pergamum -- *Some churches and Christians will think they can be more effective sharing God's light if they compromise with the darkness by making darkness feel comfortable in their midst. When darkness is comfortable with the light, the light has ceased to shine.*

Thyatira -- *The devil will tempt Christians to think they can believe in Jesus in their heart and live like unbelievers in their life, trying to be light and darkness at the same time. Some will even think this "experience" with the darkness will make them more effective as lights. Others will contend that such behavior does not damage the light or their relationship with God. Light that looks like darkness is darkness!*

Sardis -- *Satan will convince some churches and some Christians to substitute service to themselves in place of service to God, working for their personal benefit and improvement rather than living to honor and serve God. Their works will appear as light when in God's eyes they will be darkness.*

Philadelphia -- *Growth is God's business. God alone can give an "open door" to the work of sharing his light. We will see God use some churches and Christians to "harvest" his plentiful crop. These "lampstands" under God's blessing will find acceptance and growth as they shine God's light in this world. That growth comes from God alone, not from the skill of those who present the light.*

Laodicea -- *The most insidious attack the darkness will bring against the lampstands is the darkness of apathy. Satan will tempt Christians to think the faith in their hearts requires no action in their lives. Those who fall prey to this attack will devote their time and energy to their desires and plans while having no time or energy to serve God. We will see "lukewarm" Christians who are too busy to worship God or to serve him, all the while claiming they love God and that he is first with them.*

CHAPTER SEVEN
The Vision of the Seven Seals

Revelation Chapters 4-7

Introduction

The first visions of the Revelation revealed our purpose in this world. We are God's "lampstands" entrusted with God's light and chosen by God to share that light with the dark world around us. God also shaped our "lampstand expectations" with the Vision of the Seven Letters, preparing us for the fact that the darkness will oppose the light we offer. The Vision of the Seven Seals, recorded in Revelation chapters four to seven, reveals what it will be like to live in this world until Jesus comes again. This is the next truth we need to understand.

What God reveals as he opens the Seven Seals confirms the warning God issued in the book of Acts. *...We must go through many hardships to enter the kingdom of God.* (Acts 14:22 NIV) God reveals the nature and the extent of the hardship all people will face until Jesus comes again as he opens the Seven Seals. In the curse God pronounced on Adam at the dawn of time, God stated that the ground would produce thorns and thistles and would work against Adam every day. Since that day all creation has groaned under the burden of that curse. The Vision of the Seven Seals paints the picture of how that curse affects the lives of every person on this earth.

God begins the story of that vision by taking us into heaven where we see God seated on his throne. From there God will reveal to us what is going to happen in this world until Christ comes again.

Nothing is an accident in this world. Nothing happens in this universe unless God allows it. Above all, all things play some role in God's eternal and ancient plan for this world. God is sharing his message of light with all people before Jesus comes again. Every event in this world originates from God's throne and serves the purpose of God's eternal plan.

However, the Vision of the Seven Letters to the Seven Churches showed us that there is a problem. We live in a world where people love the darkness and hate the light. Many live in open rebellion against God. As a result of this rebellion, God is forced to pour out mini-judgments on the world each day to deal with those who rebel against him. God intends these judgments to act as warnings to the world to repent before it is too late.

These two facts together form the context of what we are about to see. God is reaching out to all people with this light. At the same time, God is revealing his wrath to those who walk the path of rebellion against him. The Vision of the Seven Seals reveals the confluence of these two cross purposes and the effect this confluence has on life in this world for all people.

Read Revelation 4:1-11

THE THRONE OF GOD

If we are going to understand what is happening in this world, the place to begin is in heaven. Therefore in the Vision of the Seven Seals, God begins by inviting us to enter the holy ground of heaven. As John enters heaven, his eyes are drawn at once to a huge throne. On that throne God himself is seated and from that throne God is ruling the universe. This is the first thing you have to know about this world. It may appear to be driven by chaos with no discernible plan, but the truth is, there is a God in heaven right now. This God is not just a spectator. At this moment he is ruling the world every day and he is using his power to carry out his plan to bring light to the world filled with darkness.

John saw that God was not alone. Circling the throne of God were 24 other thrones and on those were seated 24 elders. Remember that twelve is the number of the church. God uses this number in the Revelation to remind us that he is caring for his church every day, either revealing a promise he makes to his church or he is showing the fulfillment of a promise. Here the 24 elders represent the full church of God from the Old and the New Testament. Think about the twelve tribes of Old Testament Israel and the twelve apostles chosen by the Lord in the New Testament. God promised his people that one day they would rule with him in heaven. *Jesus said to them, "I tell you the truth, at the renewal of all things ... you who have followed me will also sit on twelve thrones, judging the twelve tribes of Israel."* (Matt. 19:28 NIV) *Do you not know that the saints will judge the world?* (1 Cor. 6:2 NIV) Here God shows that promise fulfilled in the form of the church of God seated on thrones in heaven ruling with the Lord.

As the vision continues, John sees four amazing creatures surrounding God's throne. Each one had a unique face. One had the face of a lion. The second had the face of an ox. The third had the face of a man. The fourth had the face of an eagle. John tells us these strange creatures had six wings and they were covered with eyes. These mysterious creatures stand before God's throne giving him their full attention. While God does not identify the "living creatures" in the Revelation, we can discover what the creatures were by following our second Bible reading principle. We can let Scripture interpret itself. In this case it turns out that Isaiah and Ezekiel in the Old Testament both had visions of heaven and both saw these same living creatures. Ezekiel describes them in much the same way as John. Later in his book, Ezekiel identifies the four creatures. *These were the living creatures I had seen beneath the God of Israel by the Kebar River, and I realized that they were cherubim.* (Ezek. 10:20 NIV)

From this we can confidently say that the four living creatures John saw in front of God's throne in heaven were a special rank of angels called cherubim. Noting this, suddenly the Old Testament pictures of heaven come into focus. This is why God commanded that the Tabernacle and the Ark of the Covenant and Solomon's Temple be decorated with cherubim. Such places of worship on earth provide sinful human beings with an entry into the presence of God. In heaven cherubim are always present before God's throne. The cherubim play a significant role in carrying out God's will in this world.

The final thing that stands out in this vision of heaven is that, at this moment, the creatures before the throne of God were in the midst of a huge celebration. Led by the four cherubim, all in heaven bow before the throne of God and proclaim his holiness and his worthiness. God had won an amazing victory and all of heaven was celebrating the moment. The key to understanding the cause of the celebration is to identify the day on which it takes place. This God reveals in chapter five of the Revelation as he continues to paint the picture of the Vision of the Seven Seals.

Read Revelation 5:1-14

THE LION, THE LAMB, AND THE SCROLL

To answer the question of "when" the celebration in heaven took place, God introduces us to a new vision. We call it the Vision of the Lion, the Lamb, and the Scroll. As John focuses his attention on God sitting on the throne, he notices a new detail. *Then I saw in the right hand of him who sat on the throne a scroll with writing on both sides and sealed with seven seals.* (Rev. 5:1 NIV) It is obvious to John that the scroll in God's hand is the reason he is there. It contains information everyone in the world is going to need. But there is a problem. ... *no one in heaven or on earth or under the earth could open the scroll or even look inside it.* (Rev. 5:3 NIV) When no one is able to open the scroll and the vital information remains hidden, John is filled with sorrow. This scroll contains information God's people need and no one is able to provide it.

Then one of the elders on the 24 thrones urges John to dry his tears. A new figure is entering heaven. *Then one of the elders said to me, "Do not weep! See, the Lion of the tribe of Judah, the Root of David, has triumphed. He is able to open the scroll and its seven seals."* (Rev. 5:5 NIV) The elder calls him the Lion of Judah. Suddenly John sees a Lamb standing before the throne. The Lamb is ... *looking as if it had been slain ... He had seven horns and seven eyes.* (Rev. 5:6 NIV) This Lamb is a picture of Jesus. Be sure to notice two things about this Lamb. First note that the Lamb was *"... looking as if it had been slain."* This description helps us fix this moment in time. Jesus enters heaven after the events of Good Friday and Easter Sunday. Also note that John sees that the Lamb is marked in the vision with the number seven, the number of the Gospel Covenant. What John is witnessing is a momentous "covenant event," something connected with the central purpose God is carrying out in this world. The number seven alerts us to this fact. Then the Lamb does something that changes everything. *He came and took the scroll from the right hand of him who sat on the throne.* (Rev. 5:7 NIV) When he does, all the creatures of heaven burst into praise.

This was the moment for which all creation had been waiting. Their words of praise tell the story of the celebration and the day. *You are worthy to take the scroll and to open its seals, because you were slain, and with your blood you purchased men for God from every tribe and language and people and nation.* (Rev. 5:9 NIV) Jesus won the favor of God for all of sinful mankind. He did this by taking their place and dying the death all people deserved. Now the debt is paid. The beings of heaven sing, *You have made them to be a kingdom and priests to serve our God, and they will reign on the earth.* (Rev. 5:10 NIV) Instead of facing the wrath of God, now all people in Christ are treasures to God. All who believe in Jesus are members of God's kingdom. They have the access of a priest to God himself. They will reign with the Lord forever.

We are witnessing what happened in heaven the day the disciples saw the Lord ascend. This is a vision of Ascension Day in heaven. As the clouds hid the Lord from their sight on earth, this is the scene that transpired on the other side of those clouds in heaven. God reveals this scene to us to help us understand what is happening and will happen in our world. God already showed us that he allows the world to continue to exist each day because of the light. God is reaching as many people as possible with the news of what he has done. Now he goes further and shows us that this is a plan which God has been carrying out ever since the Garden of Eden. There God promised Adam and Eve a Savior would come. Now Jesus came and lived and died and rose again for us. By this act, Jesus gained the victory God promised. This victory made it possible for the Lord to take the next step, to open the seals on the scroll of the future and to carry out the plan to make his enemies his footstool. This is what we are seeing in our world until Christ comes again. God turns our attention to what will happen in this world as he defeats his enemies with the victory he won while bringing his people safely to heaven. God tells this story in the Vision of the Seven Seals.

Read Revelation 6:1-17

THE SEVEN SEALS OF GOD

> **Psalm 110:1** *The LORD says to my Lord: "Sit at my right hand until I make your enemies a footstool for your feet."*

> **1 Corinthians 15:25,26** *For he must reign until he has put all his enemies under his feet.* [26] *The last enemy to be destroyed is death.*

God begins the Vision of the Seven Seals with a broad picture of heaven. A huge celebration is taking place there as the Lamb of God enters heaven victorious. As chapter four and five continue, the focus of the vision narrows to a scroll that God holds in his hand as he sits on the throne. That scroll contains information we desperately need if we are going to live in this world. The scroll tells the story of our future. The Lamb, by winning the victory, is able to open the scroll and the history is set to begin. Chapter six of the Revelation tells the story.

The Vision of the Seven Seals reveals six troubling things that will be true for every age of this world until Jesus comes again. Taken together these six truths tell everyone on earth that something is terribly wrong between God and the universe he created. The wars and famines and disease and disasters serve as daily spiritual warning signs. These signs are both judgments on the world in rebellion against God and warnings to repent before the greater judgment yet to come happens.

As the picture continues in Revelation chapter six, the seminal moment has come, the moment for which John wept. God is about to show us what life will be like in this world for God's lampstands and for all people as we journey through a world that loves darkness. As we fix our eyes on this new picture from the Lord, we stand on the threshold of the future. We are going to learn things we need to know if we are going to be prepared to live in this world and to understand what we see.

From the Vision of Christ Among the Lampstands, we know that God has a plan for this world and that he is carrying out that plan every day. God is sharing his message of light with the whole world before it is too late. God uses us as instruments to carry out his plan. We are lampstands for the Lord shining his light into the darkness. The Vision of the Seven Letters to the Seven Churches revealed that the darkness will hate the light and oppose the plan of God. This forces the Lord to deal with the rebellion at the same time he is reaching out with his mercy.

Revelation tells the story of the consequences of the rebellion and how God daily warns the world to repent before it is too late. The continuing judgments of God, visible in this world and predicted in the Revelation, will be frightening to see even for believers. For this reason as we begin our look at the Vision of the Seven Seals, we need to remember that all the beings in heaven burst into celebration when God put his plan in motion on Ascension Day. In the plan of God, even God's judgment on his enemies is cause for great joy and celebration as God reaches out to the world with his mercy. *Surely your (God's) wrath against men brings you praise...* (Psalm 76:10 NIV)

The Vision of the Seven Seals makes one clear point. Everything that happens in this world originates from the throne of God. The Lamb is the one opening the seals and directing the events that occur. The blessings we see in the seals come from the Lord as he aids his lampstands in reaching out with his light. The judgments we see in the seals come from the Lord as he afflicts his enemies with his wrath while warning them to repent before the great day of judgment comes upon them. Both the blessings and the judgments are part of God's plan for this world, and both will continuously occur until Jesus comes again. All people on this earth will see the six seals in their lives until Jesus returns.

As the Lamb opens the first seal John sees a White Horse ride into the world. God tells us its rider wears a crown, carries a battle bow, and rides as a conqueror through the pages of history. God does not tell us what the horse represents. This fact gives us another opportunity to apply our second Bible reading principle, namely, that the Bible interprets itself. We find that this White Horse and its rider appear again in Revelation 19:13. There God identifies the rider as *"... the Word of God."* We know from the Gospel of John that Jesus is called *"the Word."* Therefore God identifies the rider of the White Horse as Jesus.

Putting the pictures together, the first thing God tells us about the future of this world is this. From the first coming to the second coming of Jesus, God will send the White Horse of the Gospel riding throughout the world. Everyone will see this horse and its rider. God will make sure that the message of the Savior is heard in every age as he tries to reach as many people as possible before it is too late.

We should note that some Christians struggle with this understanding of the White Horse. What troubles them is that the Seven Seals reveal five terrible judgments all will see in this world. The White Horse is the only "good news" in the vision. This causes some to think that, for the sake of a uniform message, the first seal must also reveal a dark judgment of God's wrath. For this reason some Christians begin to guess at what judgment the White Horse might represent. We will see this pattern often as people study the Revelation. Many will be more than eager to supply guesses from their active imaginations to explain the symbols within the book. The result of their efforts will be much confusion about the meaning of God's pictures. We will not take part in that confusion. Our plan from the start is to let *"Scripture interpret Scripture."* When God tells us in Revelation 19 that Jesus rides the White Horse, we are content to believe that this is the same White Horse we find in Revelation chapter six. This approach allows God to interpret what he writes and keeps us from providing our own guesses for what we see.

As the Lamb opens the second seal, John sees a fiery Red Horse ride out. God tells us that this is the Red Horse of War. It carries the terrible power of the sword which it uses to *"take peace from the earth"* and to *"make men slay each other."* The violence we see in our world, the wars, people killing other people, are all sightings of the Red Horse. These are visible signs on the surface of our lives revealing the wrath of the Lord. Jesus sends the Red Horse to warn the darkness to repent before it is too late. Those who do not heed the Red Horse will face a greater terror on the Day of Judgment. Throughout the time from the first to the second coming of Jesus, those who walk the earth in every age will see this horse of war and murder riding through the streets and the back yards of every nation.

When he opens the third seal, the Lamb releases the Black Horse to ride into the New Testament times. John sees a pair of scales in the rider's hand and hears a voice announce prices for food that are so expensive, no one can afford them. The Black Horse represents economic hardship. Depressions, famines, recessions, panics and crashes are not accidents. They are spiritual events pregnant with messages from God warning of his wrath and urging repentance now, before it is too late. Everyone who lives until Jesus comes again will see this Black Horse ride in their life. And always it will carry a warning from the Lord. The Gospel of John warns us to *"love not the world or anything in the world."* Jesus told parables which warned against the dangers posed by the *"deceitfulness of wealth"* which promises security but delivers none. The economic hardship brought by the Black Horse announces the coming wrath of God to those in darkness while warning God's believers to put their trust in the Lord rather than in earthly wealth.

The Lamb revealed the Pale Horse riding into the world when he opened the fourth seal. The rider of this horse was called "death" and the Pale Horse carries the warning of the graveyard. Until Jesus comes again all people will see this Pale Horse ride in their lives. His appearance comes in the form of sickness and accidents and other tragedies which result in death. People of every age find themselves attending funerals and visiting graveyards and experiencing loss as the Pale Horse rides through their lives. Leaving sorrow and loss in his wake, the Pale Horse announces to all mankind that life is temporary. There is a Day of Judgment coming for every person. Repent now before it is too late.

With the fifth seal, the Lamb turns our attention to a scene in heaven. John sees "souls," people whose bodies have died. Pay careful attention to John's exact words ... *under the altar the souls of those who had been slain because of the word of God and the testimony they had maintained.* (Rev. 6:9 NIV) These are believers in the New Testament whose lives were cut short by persecution. Now in heaven they cry out to the Lord for justice with the words *"how long?"* The

Lord counsels patience as he tells them to ... *wait a little longer, until the number of their fellow servants and brothers who were to be killed as they had been was completed.* (Rev. 6:9 NIV) This fifth seal reveals a truth that has special application to those who carry the light of the Lord in this world. Even as the world hated Jesus and hung him on a cross, so the world will hate and persecute those who follow the Lord. Believers will suffer scorn and persecution from the world until Jesus returns again. God reveals in the fifth seal that even this terrible reality has a place in God's plan.

As the sixth seal opens John sees the end of all things revealed "from the perspective of the unbeliever." This is the constant growing shadow that will hang over the world for the entire New Testament era. Jesus is coming again. There are two parts to this picture. First John witnesses the destruction of the universe as the Lord of heaven and earth appears on the last day. Every part of the universe -- the earth, the sun, the moon, the stars, even the sky -- is destroyed at one time. As this occurs, John watches the people of this world react with terror in their hearts. You can hear the terror in their words. *They called to the mountains and the rocks, "Fall on us and hide us from the face of him who sits on the throne and from the wrath of the Lamb!"* (Rev. 6:16 NIV) As the cataclysmic events of that last day unfold before their eyes, all the rebellious people in the world will realize they are facing the wrath of the Lamb. In terror they will cry out for a way to escape, and they will not find one. And so this world will come to an end.

The six truths revealed in the Vision of the Seven Seals terrify the hearts of all who live on this earth, even the children of God. For this reason, God concludes this section of the Revelation with a vision meant to reassure and comfort his people. We find that final panel of the Vision of the Seven Seals recorded in chapter seven of the book of Revelation.

Read Revelation 7:1-17

The Vision of the Seven Seals reveals a path of hardship and challenge for all people. That is unsettling, especially for Christians. This is why God concludes the Vision of the Seven Seals with two closing visions of comfort. The first is the Vision of the 144,000 marked with the seal of God on their foreheads. This vision begins with four angels armed with the power of the *"four winds"* to bring harm to the earth. Then another angel appears commanding the four angels to hold back from the damage they intend. John watches as this angel marks the people of God with God's seal on their foreheads. Notice that the 144,000 are located on earth facing a future of living among the seven seals. God's seal on their foreheads will keep them safe from the calamities brought about by God's wrath.

The second thing to notice is the number God uses to identify this group. Remember that twelve is the number of the church of God in the Revelation. When God uses that number or its multiples, God is always either revealing a promise to his church or he is fulfilling a promise to his church. Here we see the number twelve squared to equal 144. The number 144,000 combines the number twelve with the number ten. 1,000 is ten cubed. We have already seen how God uses the number ten in the Revelation. Each time he is representing the concept of "completeness." Combining the number ten with the number twelve to equal 144,000, God is picturing his complete church on earth, all the believers who will live their lives in the midst of the seven seals. Even as God pours out his mini-judgments on this earth, the believers can be assured God will keep them from harm.

It is important to note that God does not promise the actions of the Red Horse and the Black Horse and the Pale Horse will not affect the lives of those who believe in Jesus. God already revealed that these horses will ride through the lives of every person on earth. God tells us that *"a righteous man may have many troubles ..."* However those who have the seal of God on their foreheads can trust that even when hardship comes, God will turn that hardship into a blessing for his children. *"And we know that in all things God works for the good of those who love him, who have been called according to his purpose."* (Rom. 8:28 NIV) This is the assurance the seal of the Lord gives to believers as they travel through the wilderness of life in this dangerous world.

Next John sees a huge numberless multitude dressed in white robes. It is important to recognize that the *"great multitude that no one can count"* is the same group of people which John observed in the Vision of the 144,000. However the second group is standing in heaven before the Lamb and the throne of God. Here there is no more danger or threat. The war is over and God's church is safe just as he promised. Now as they stand before the throne of God enjoying the fulfillment of God's promise to keep them safe, all of heaven breaks into joyful celebration of the promises God has fulfilled. *And they cried out in a loud voice: "Salvation belongs to our God, who sits on the throne, and to the Lamb."* (Rev. 7:10 NIV) Their song goes on to rejoice in the security heaven offers for eternity from the effects of sin and judgment. *Never again will they hunger; never again will they thirst. The sun will not beat upon them, nor any scorching heat. [17]For the Lamb at the center of the throne will be their shepherd; he will lead them to springs of living water. And God will wipe away every tear from their eyes.* (Rev. 7:16,17 NIV)

Revelation chapter seven brings the Vision of the Seven Seals to a conclusion. The lessons God teaches with this vision are critical for us to learn if we are going to carry out our purpose as God's lampstands in this world. God makes it very clear that he is in control of all that happens. The seals all originate from the throne of God by the hand of the Lamb. From there God strengthens and supports his people in their work with the White Horse. Also from that same throne God issues the warnings of his mini-judgments, revealing his wrath to the unbelieving world. Taken together, God reveals a challenging future which Paul once described with these words. *We must go through many hardships to enter the kingdom of God.* (Acts 14:22 NIV)

While this truth is surprising and challenging for God's people, fix your attention daily on these two thoughts. First of all, as terrible as many of the images are in the Vision of the Seven Seals, remember that there are "seven" seals. God uses that number to remind us that what we are seeing in the vision, even the most terrible things, somehow play a part in God's plan to reach the world with his light. The second thing to keep in mind is the sure and certain destination which God has prepared for those who follow him. God concludes the Vision of the Seals with these final pictures of safety and eternal care. We walk through a dangerous world and we will all see the terrifying horses and the sorrow they bring. But we will be safe through it all, because God has marked us with his seal. He is watching over us and he will make all things work for our good. God's promise of safety and blessing is certain for all believers on this earth. *A righteous man may have many troubles, but the LORD delivers him from them all.* (Psalm 34:19) While we walk through this earth in that security, we do so knowing that our future is equally secure. God has promised us a place at his side in heaven. He urges us to fix our eyes on that destination every day. When our journey is complete and all is said and done *"God … will spread his tent over them."*

Chapter Summary

The Third Essential Revelation Truth

All people will suffer hardship in life due to the curse of sin as God shows his judgment to unbelievers while reaching out to all people with the Gospel.

God reveals what the believer and the unbeliever will experience as they journey through life in a world cursed by sin!

> **Romans 8:22,23** *We know that the whole creation has been groaning as in the pains of childbirth right up to the present time.* [23] *Not only so, but we ourselves, who have the firstfruits of the Spirit, groan inwardly as we wait eagerly for our adoption as sons, the redemption of our bodies.* (NIV)

> **Acts 14:22** *. ...We must go through many hardships to enter the kingdom of God.* (NIV)

> **Job 5:7** *Yet man is born to trouble as surely as sparks fly upward.* (NIV)

> **Psalm 34:19** *A righteous man may have many troubles, but the LORD delivers him from them all.* (NIV)

The Vision of the Seven Seals *reveals the truth that life in this world will be filled with trials and hardship, for unbelievers and especially for God's children. The four horses will ride through the backyards of every person in this world. All will see the White Horse preaching the Gospel, the Red Horse bringing war and murder, the Black Horse bringing economic hardship, and the Pale Horse bringing death from sickness and accident and tragedy. Christians will face persecution in this world because they are God's lampstands. Finally, the world* *will come to an end with great suffering and terror filling the hearts of unbelievers. Even though God assures us in Ps.4:3 "... the LORD has set apart the godly for himself." God wants his people to be prepared for the difficult journey that is life in a world cursed by sin.*

Revelation chapters four and five *reveal that God is in control of all that happens in this world. Starting on Ascension Day, God began the task of administering the victory Jesus won on Easter Sunday, namely putting all his enemies under his feet. Note that the horses ride out from the throne of God.*

Revelation chapter seven *uses two visions of God's people, one on earth and one in heaven, to assure believers that God has placed his mark on them. Therefore believers can take comfort in knowing that even in a difficult and dangerous world, God will watch over them and keep them safe.*

CHAPTER EIGHT
The Vision of the Seven Trumpets of Judgment: Part One

Revelation Chapter 8 & 9

Psalm 7:11 *God is a righteous judge, a God who expresses his wrath every day.* (NIV)

Many of us follow the same ritual as we walk through each new day on this earth. We pay attention to the news around us either by reading a newspaper or by watching the news on television. The story the news tells is always the same. The headlines tell of tragedies and atrocities and accidents, stories of suffering and loss. There seems to be no rhyme or reason to it, just visible daily chaos. God wrote the Vision of the Seven Trumpets of Judgment to open our eyes to the pattern which explains what we see each day. There is a pattern and an explanation for all that we see. We can understand what is happening. According to the new vision God presents in Revelation chapters eight and nine, all we need are *"trumpet lessons,"* specifically lessons in the Seven Trumpets of Judgment.

In these lessons God will also address another troubling question that grew out of our study of the Vision of the Seven Seals. As we watched the Lamb open one seal after another, we could not help but notice that the horses rode into everyone's backyard, believer and unbeliever alike. All people are touched by the tragedies of war and violence and economic hardship and death. It appears from the Vision of the

Seven Seals that the Lord treats believers and unbelievers alike. God addresses that conclusion in the Vision of the Seven Trumpets. Here God will teach us that the unbelievers in this world have a very different experience from the believers. The more skillful we become at hearing the trumpets, the more clearly we will understand this new truth.

So let the trumpet lessons begin. When God is finished training our spiritual ears to hear the trumpets blow, we will understand this world in a whole new way. This vision is one of the longer lessons in the Revelation. For this reason we will cover the vision in two chapters. First we will study Revelation chapters eight and nine in part one. Then in the next chapter we will study Revelation chapters ten and eleven in part two.

Read Revelation 8:1-13

The First Four Trumpets

One key to keep in mind as we study the pictures of the Revelation is "God's thought progression" as he moves from one vision to the next. God is revealing a set of truths with the pictures of the Revelation and these truths are related to one another. In fact, each new truth grows out of and in response to the truths that came before. Taken together, all the truths comprise a complete set of essential information that prepares the Christian to live in this world with understanding and with confidence. This revealed knowledge equips the Christian to fulfill his purpose every day.

Consider God's thought progression so far. The first thought or truth that God revealed is his purpose each day in this world. God wants to share his message of light with all people, before it is too late. We are the lampstands or instruments God uses in this endeavor. That thought leads us to the next truth. In the Vision of the Seven Letters God revealed that his lampstands would face opposition and persecution from the dark world as the lampstands try to share God's light. It is surprising that a world which needs the light so badly would so stridently oppose that light. Then in the Vision of the Seven Seals God introduced the next thought, namely that all people would find tribulation and hardship on the path of life in a world cursed by sin. These truths have been difficult to hear. However, we must remember that there were seven letters and seven seals. God uses the number seven to remind us that even though some visions show terrible sights, God is using even the hardest moments to accomplish the purpose of his Gospel Covenant.

The hardship which believers and unbelievers experience as revealed by the seals leads directly to the next thought which God addresses in the Vision of the Seven Trumpets. Here God will show us that the experience of the unbeliever in this world is entirely different from that of the believer. Keep "God's thought progression" clearly in mind as you walk through the picture gallery that is the book of Revelation.

With the first verses of chapter eight, God begins the Vision of the Seven Trumpets of Judgment. God uses this vision to take us further into the discussion of life in this sin-cursed world. With the Trumpets of Judgment God adds a new truth as he addresses a nagging question caused by the Vision of the Seven Seals. It is the question Abraham placed before the Lord as he pleaded with God to spare the cities of Sodom and Gomorrah. *Will you really... kill the righteous with the wicked, treating the righteous and the wicked alike?* (Gen. 18:24-26 NIV)

We can't help but notice as we watch the Vision of the Seven Seals unfold that all the people of the earth, believers and unbelievers alike, were affected by the seals. The Red Horse of War rides through the lives of believer and unbeliever. The Black Horse of economic hardship destroys the job of the Christian as well as the job of the unbeliever. The Pale Horse of disease and death brings illness to the lives of child of God and child of Satan without discrimination. In the face of this reality, the believers ask the Lord the question of Abraham. *"Do you treat the righteous and the wicked alike?"*

Worse than that, the Vision of the Seven Seals revealed that the believers have an even harder road to travel. Not only must believers endure the same hardships all people face in this world. The believers' lives are also made harder by persecution from the unbelievers. Under this terrible added burden the martyred saints cried out to the Lord under the fifth seal, *"How long?"*

In the Vision of the Seven Trumpets of Judgment the Lord provides his answer. The Vision of the Seven Trumpets begins with the ending of the Vision of the Seven Seals. The seventh seal is opened and the throng in heaven responds with breath taking silence. This lasts for half an hour. Then John sees *"another angel"* who carries a censer in his hand. John describes the scene in these words. *Another angel, who had a golden censer, came and stood at the altar. He was given much incense to offer, with the prayers of all the saints, on the golden altar before the throne. ⁴ The smoke of the incense, together with the prayers of the saints, went up before God from the angel's hand.* (Rev. 8:3,4 NIV) God hears our question and now will show us his answer. The action of the angel portends what is to come. *Then the angel took the censer, filled it with fire from the altar, and hurled it on the earth; and there came peals of thunder, rumblings, flashes of lightning and an earthquake.* (Rev. 8:5 NIV)

The censer filled with fire is the Lord's answer. The Trumpets of Judgment will carry the message that God does not treat the believer and the unbeliever the same on this earth. The experience each has is entirely different one from the other. The difference is the judgment and wrath of the Lord. As we read the elements of this new vision, we must keep in mind that all we see here is in the context of an answer to the prayers of the believers. On the surface it may appear that the believer and the unbeliever share common sorrow and hardship on this earth. However the judgment and impending wrath of the Lord lies buried within the sorrow and loss the unbeliever encounters. There is no such wrath of the Lord in any experience the believer has.

Consider the experience of King Jeroboam of Israel. As a sign of God's wrath to him, God allowed the evil king's son to die. However, while the loss of the child was a sign of God's anger with the evil king, the death the child experienced was a sign of God's grace to that child. *All Israel will mourn for him and bury him. He is the only one belonging to Jeroboam who will be buried, because he is the only one in the house of Jeroboam in whom the LORD, the God of Israel, has found anything good.* (1 Kings 14:13 NIV) The prophet Isaiah makes the same observation regarding the death of God's children. *The righteous perish, and no one ponders it in his heart; devout men are taken away, and no one understands that the righteous are taken away to be spared from evil. ²Those who walk uprightly enter into peace; they find rest as they lie in death.* (Isaiah 57:1,2 NIV) For those who dare to walk this earth in open rebellion against the Lord, the people of the Broken Covenant, the wrath of the Lord begins on this earth and builds to a horrible end. For the unbeliever every hardship and every sorrow is a message from the Lord, a warning of a greater judgment to come in the shadow of the approaching Lord. This is the tale told by the Seven Trumpets of Judgment.

The angel continues to pour out the fire of the censer of God's judgment on the earth and each new trumpet heralds another sign of God's wrath poured out upon the unbeliever. God tells us in the first four trumpets that we will not have to search for these warning signs. They will be present on every plane of our existence. To understand the message, we must realize that the trumpets in general, and the first four in particular, are metaphors. Each is a picture telling us where we will see the judgment of the Lord on the unbeliever, the visible sign of the Lord's impending wrath. As we walk through each day of our journey on this earth, God urges his people to listen for the trumpets.

Keep the timeframe of the Revelation in mind. With each new vision

God is teaching us new truths that apply to the entire period of time between the first and the second coming of Christ. So it is with each of the trumpets and the warnings they carry. The first angel blows the trumpet and calls our attention to the earth. *The first angel sounded his trumpet, and there came hail and fire mixed with blood, and it was hurled down upon the earth. A third of the earth was burned up, a third of the trees were burned up, and all the green grass was burned up.* (Rev. 8:7 NIV) As we walk this earth, we will see God's wrath revealed in many disasters against the people of the Broken Covenant. From horrific accidents by cars and trains and buses, to frightening disasters by storms and earthquakes, to the terrifying horror and destruction that man brings to the earth as he wars with his fellowman, we will see tragic loss of life and horrible suffering. These disasters happen to believer and unbeliever alike. That is what the world sees. However, the child of God knows better. Hardship in an unbeliever's life carries a message from God announcing to the unbeliever that something is wrong between him and God. For the believer there is no such message from the Lord. Instead, the believer faces every challenge with confidence. He knows that God will make all things work for his good, turning even painful moments into blessings. Therefore, in those moments of calamity and disaster on this earth, while the world in agony wonders why these things happen, God's children will hear the first trumpet blowing and we will understand. The first angel is blowing his trumpet and we are witnessing the Lord's judgment, a call to all in rebellion to repent before it is too late.

When the second angel sounds his trumpet, John sees the wrath of God revealed on the sea. A huge mountain falls into the sea, and one third of the sea turns to blood. The oceans of the world can be places of terrible danger. They can also be forces capable of causing huge destruction. It is common to hear of loss of life and property in connection with the oceans of the world. When Christians read of such events, giant ships that sink with great loss of life, the great floods that destroy life and property, and the individual incidents where life is harmed or lost, we are hearing the second angel sound his trumpet. God is sounding the warning to unbelievers in each of these moments small and large that a great judgment is coming.

The third angel's trumpet calls John's attention to the fresh waters of the earth with the same warning. John sees a giant star fall from the sky, a star called *"Wormwood."* This star falls into the fresh water of the earth and a third of the water turns bitter. The result is that many people who drink this water die. Again the message is one of judgment for unbelievers. God's impending wrath against the rebellious mankind turns fresh water into an implement of destruction. In every disaster on lakes and rivers, with every loss of life and property, God is revealing his wrath to the rebellious world and warning of a great judgment to come.

When the fourth angel blows his trumpet, God reveals that his wrath will be visible even in the heavens. John sees …*a third of the sun was struck, a third of the moon, and a third of the stars, so that a third of them turned dark. A third of the day was without light, and also a third of the night.* (Rev. 8:7 NIV) The fourth trumpet reveals that no place in the universe is safe from the wrath of God. Everywhere the unbeliever goes and everywhere he looks, he will hear the angels blowing their trumpets. Here the destruction and judgment of God appears in the heavens. Perhaps God is describing events such as meteors striking the earth with accompanying loss of life or perhaps God is describing the negative and harmful influences the sun and the other planetary bodies may have on the earth over time. God uses the metaphor of "darkness" to convey the meaning. As one third of the earth suffers from the darkness of the fourth trumpet, God reveals even here his judgment on those who dare to rebel against him.

Following the fourth trumpet, John sees a new ominous sight warning of even more terrible signs of God's wrath ahead. An eagle flies through the sky and the eagle carries a warning for those who walk this earth in the Broken Covenant. *"Woe! Woe! Woe to the inhabitants* of the earth, because of the trumpet blasts about to be sounded by the other three angels!" (Rev. 8:13 NIV) If we thought the terror and judgment announced in the first four trumpets was devastating, the eagle's words tell us the worst is yet to come. Unbelievers will not go unpunished. God is not ignoring their actions. The sound of the trumpets is everywhere warning that the wrath of God is present and approaching. God is answering the prayers of his people.

As we conclude our study of Revelation chapter eight, we must make sure we clearly understand the truth God is presenting. The first four trumpets reveal that God's wrath will be visible everywhere in this universe until Jesus returns. *God is a righteous judge, a God who expresses his wrath every day.* (Psalm 7:11 NIV) All people will see the signs of this wrath in the disastrous events that occur. We will see ships that sink, planes and cars and trains that crash, and floods and famine and fire that overwhelm and destroy people.

It is a fact that these disasters affect Christians and unbelievers alike. The Vision of the Seven Seals makes that clear. But that fact does not change the truth that what the unbeliever experiences in a disaster or illness is not the same thing that a child of God experiences in the same hardship. This is the point God is making with the Vision of the Trumpets. Disaster or illness will come to a believer's life. But that disaster does not separate the believer from the love of God. *For I am convinced that neither death nor life, neither angels nor demons, neither the present nor the future, nor any powers,* [39] *neither height nor depth, nor anything else in all creation, will be able to separate us from the love of God that is in Christ Jesus our Lord.* (Rom. 8:38,39 NIV) No matter what occurs in the life of a child of God, he knows that God is with him and all is well. The believer lives confident that God will turn even the most severe trial into a blessing.

The unbeliever confronts a very different reality when enduring the same hardship. For the unbeliever, God embeds in each new trial the clear warning of his impending wrath and judgment. The disaster in his life reminds the unbeliever that something is terribly wrong between him and God. Worse than that is the uneasy feeling that a greater disaster is coming. The wrath of God makes the experience of hardships for the unbeliever very different from the experience a believer has in what appears to be the same trial. For example, both the believer and the unbeliever may lose their job. In that moment the believer looks forward with hope and confidence to tomorrow. He knows God loves him and God will provide for him. The unbeliever has no such confidence. For him the loss of his job is the trumpet of judgment blowing, warning him of God's wrath and urging him to repent before a more terrible judgment comes upon him. This is the truth God is revealing in the Vision of the Trumpets of Judgment. That truth becomes clearer as the final trumpets begin to blow.

Read Revelation 9:1-21

THE LAST THREE TRUMPETS OF JUDGMENT

In chapter nine the fifth angel blows his trumpet and God clarifies the new truth he is revealing. As the trumpet blows, John sees a *"star that had fallen from the sky"* and this *"star was given the key to the ... Abyss."* The star is the devil. We know that by his next action. He takes the key and opens the Abyss. When he does, *"smoke rose from it like the smoke of a gigantic furnace."*

When the Abyss of hell is opened smoke rises, smoke so dense that the sun and the sky are darkened. Out of this smoke came a new terrible sight. Locusts! These creatures had the power to harm people, but that power is reserved for one group of people only. John is told that the locusts can harm *"...only those people who did not have the seal of God on their foreheads."* (Rev. 9:4 NIV) This is the new truth God reveals in the Vision of the Trumpets of Judgment. The fifth trumpet shows us that God is setting the unbelievers apart to experience his wrath. During the time between the first and second coming of Jesus, God is not going to ignore the evil in this world or those who carry it out. During all this time God will be pouring out his wrath and judgment into the lives of all who dare to oppose him. *God is a righteous judge, a God who expresses his wrath every day.* (Psalm 7:11 NIV)

The first four trumpets of judgment reveal that we will see the judgment of God on unbelievers everywhere we look in this world. With the fifth trumpet God reveals that his judgment on unbelievers will take a particular form. *They were not given power to kill them, but only to torture them for five months. And the agony they suffered was like that of the sting of a scorpion when it strikes a man. ⁶ During those days men will seek death, but will not find it; they will long to die, but death will elude them.* (Rev. 9:5,6 NIV) The locusts and their sting are a metaphor picturing the spiritual torment that afflicts the souls of sinners when they follow the devil's lies.

Jesus warned that the devil would attack the truth of the Gospel Covenant and its promises with powerful lies. *For false Christs and false prophets will appear and perform great signs and miracles to deceive even the elect—if that were possible.* (Matt. 24:24 NIV) The Lord described the devil and his methods in this way. *You belong to your father, the devil, and you want to carry out your father's desire. He was a murderer from the beginning, not holding to the truth, for there is no truth in him. When he lies, he speaks his native language, for he is a liar and the father of lies.* (John 8:44 NIV) The devil will not be able to prevent God's truth, the message of his Gospel Covenant, from being preached everywhere in this world. Therefore the devil will try to obscure the truth by filling the world with his lies.

We will find his lies in false man-invented religions which offer people a way to prove they deserve God's favor or to please themselves while serving God. To the false religions of the world, the devil will add the empty philosophies so common in our world: humanism, materialism, evolutionism, communism, and many others which have not risen to the "ism" status yet. The devil's lies in whatever form will cause great damage to the sin-scarred souls of men. The lies promise light but yield only darkness. They promise hope but yield only despair. Those who believe these lies will find only hopelessness. God tells John that the bite of the locusts produces despair so great ... *men will seek death, but will not find it; they will long to die, but death will elude them.* (Rev. 9:6 NIV)

Some might wonder why the lies told by Satan deceive only the unbelievers in this world. The fact is believers have a spiritual shield and a spiritual weapon protecting them from the delusions the devil offers. The weapon Christians hold is the word of God. While the world walks in darkness and is easily mislead by Satan, Christians guide their steps by what God says. *Your word is a lamp to my feet and a light for my path.* (Psalm 119:105 NIV) This light allows Christians to avoid the lies of Satan, protected by the sword of the word and the shield of faith which trusts God's word to guide them. Therefore Christians do not feel the bite of the locust. They do not believe the lies the devil tells or place their hope in such lies. As a result, Christians do not suffer the torment that comes to hearts expecting gain from the lie and finding only continued loss.

The strange truth, however, is unbelievers will continue to believe these lies, expecting contentment and happiness no matter how many times the lies prove false. Something in these locusts will be so sinister, and yet at the same time so inviting, that unbelievers will continue to believe in the lies the devil tells. John sees the locusts crowned with gold, with human faces, and endowed with the long beautiful hair of women -- all attractive traits to the people of the world. Yet the locusts have savage teeth like a lion and breastplates of iron and stings like scorpions -- all frightening features.

No matter how attractive Satan's lies are, in the end people will find only emptiness and discontent. Eventually the hopelessness fills every corner of their lives and they see no way out. They will long to die to bring their hopeless existence to an end, but death will not come soon enough for them. This is another terrible judgment which rebellious mankind will suffer on this earth until Jesus comes again. The more they embrace the lies of Satan, the more empty and hopeless their lives will become.

The locusts torment the unbelievers for *"five months."* Noting that the normal locust plague comes in cycles of five months in nature helps us to see how this number could simply be background to complete the picture of a locust plague. As locust plagues come and go on this earth, so these "spiritual locusts" will repeatedly appear and disappear on the pages of history until the Lord comes again. The devil will spawn new lies to replace old ones and the deception will continue.

But the most frightening thing John saw was the leader of this terrifying army. John says his name was *"Apollyon."* In Ephesians the Apostle Paul alerted us to the spiritual war which afflicts all people on this earth. *For our struggle is not against flesh and blood, but against the rulers, against the authorities, against the powers of this dark world and against the spiritual forces of evil in the heavenly realms.* (Eph. 6:12 NIV) The locusts and their sting reveal the wrath of God on the unbelievers of this earth. God chose to use the devil as his agent to bring about this continuing judgment. The smoke and the locusts, the lies and the false promises, all come from the devil himself. Satan brings torment to the hearts of his followers and he rejoices in their suffering. While the devil rejoices in the pain he causes, it is God's hope that those in torment will see in this suffering a warning of greater judgment to come. Perhaps then they will turn from their evil ways before it is too late.

As John watches this terrible scene, he hears even more alarming news. *Two other woes are yet to come.* With that news, the sixth trumpet blows and John hears God issue a command. *Release the four angels who are bound at the great river Euphrates.* (Rev. 9:13,14 NIV) The terrible spiritual war that is happening between the first coming of Jesus and the second will build to a climax. The sixth trumpet reveals the last terrible days on this earth just before the Lord returns. Jesus described those days in these words. *For then there will be great distress, unequaled from the beginning of the world until now—and never to be equaled again.* [22] *If those days had not been cut short, no one would survive, but for the sake of the elect those days will be shortened.* (Matt. 24:21,22 NIV) The sixth trumpet warns of those days, revealing how terrible they will be for those who walk in the darkness.

John sees a third of mankind die at that time. The lies of the devil in their many forms will fill the world with their smoke. John sees this truth in the form of a metaphor which pictured a mighty savage army that afflicts the unbelievers with terrible loss and suffering. The devil uses his lies to deceive the people of the world and to blind them to the truth of God. The more unbelievers follow the devil's lies, and the more they believe his false promises, the more they suffer. As people follow those lies and engage in the sinful and destructive behavior they advocate, those who rebel against the Lord will suffer terribly for the choices that they made. The sixth trumpet describes that suffering. But even more distressing is the reaction that the people of the Broken Covenant will have during this time of distress.

Those who love the darkness instead of the light will continue to cling to the darkness and to walk in that darkness. People will not repent of what they have done. They will not, even in those most terrible days, give up their worship of idols. Instead they will persist down the path of sin and darkness as before. In pain and suffering they will march toward the inevitable Day of Judgment when the Lord returns.

Christians living in this world must learn to listen for the sound of these trumpets. The better we get at detecting their sound, the more we will understand what our eyes see. The trumpets reveal the fact that all the disasters of this world are tied together by the wrath of God. God uses these mini-judgments to warn the dark world of his wrath so that they might repent before it is too late. The trumpets also reveal that unbelievers in this world have a much different experience as they walk through their lives. Each day God sends unbelievers messages of his wrath in the hardships they face. Believers face no such wrath. For them, all things become blessings. The basic truth of the trumpets is that unbelievers are going to face the wrath of God every day that they walk this earth.

As the earth approaches the second coming of the Lord, God's wrath, and the suffering it causes unbelievers, will only increase in those final horrible days just before the end. However, through it all, though the trumpets will be continuously blowing, the unbelievers will hear the sound but fail to discern the message they carry, and they will continue to cling to their rebellious ways. For them the wrath of God is the present and the future. This is the new truth of the Vision of the Seven Trumpets.

One last thought is worth repeating as we close our study of this somber vision. As terrible as the sound of the trumpets is, and as frightening as the message they carry may be, we must remember that there are "seven" trumpets. God is reminding us that even these terrible judgments have some role to play in God's overall plan of reaching people with his light before it is too late. Knowing this, Christians can stand in a world filled with the clarion calls of God's Seven Trumpets of Judgment and know that all is well. With Solomon we can say, God makes ... *everything beautiful in its time.* (Eccl. 3:11 NIV)

Chapter Summary

The Fourth Essential Revelation Truth

God does not treat the believer and the unbeliever the same!
The unbeliever experiences the wrath of God in every hardship.
The believer never faces God's wrath, even when he faces hardship.

God does not treat the unbeliever and the believer alike. Both will experience hardship and challenge. Both will know what it is like to lose their jobs or to get sick or to have loved ones die. However, the experience each has in those moments will be entirely different. The difference is the wrath of God. A believer may get sick or have an accident or experience a loss. Through it all he knows God is watching over him and all things will work for his good. Even hardship is a blessing in these circumstances. *A righteous man may have many troubles, but the LORD delivers him from them all.* (Psalm 34:19)

For the unbeliever the experience is much different. Every hardship, every loss, every challenge large or small, carries a message of God's wrath. The hardship is telling the unbeliever that there is something wrong between him and God. Each challenge in life is a warning from God to the unbeliever to repent now, before a greater and more terrible judgment comes upon him.

> **Ecclesiastes 3:1,11** *There is a time for everything, and a season for every activity under heaven ... He has made everything beautiful in its time.* (NIV)

> **Romans 8:28** *And we know that in all things God works for the good of those who love him, who have been called according to his purpose.* (NIV)

Romans 1:18 *The wrath of God is being revealed from heaven against all the godlessness and wickedness of men who suppress the truth by their wickedness.* (NIV)

Psalm 7:11-13 *God is a righteous judge, a God who expresses his wrath every day.* [12]*If he does not relent, he will sharpen his sword; he will bend and string his bow.* [13]*He has prepared his deadly weapons; he makes ready his flaming arrows.* (NIV)

CHAPTER NINE
The Vision of the Seven Trumpets of Judgment: Part Two

Revelation Chapters 10-11

It is pretty clear to us by now. The trumpets of God's wrath are loudly blowing in this world and everyone will hear them. The headlines in the papers and the national news at night point to their unmistakable sound. The only problem is the world fails to understand the meaning of the warning God is giving. Reporters clearly point to the trumpet's sound in the news each night. News commentators gravely report one tragedy and atrocity after another. It is clear they are all aware of the trumpets. Yet none offer the analysis that the wrath of a righteous God is being revealed against a sinful world in these events. The people in darkness persist in seeing these events as random and without spiritual meaning. They hear the sound, but they do not discern the message.

This is a disturbing picture. We are lampstands and God lets us share in the task of shining his light into the darkness. Yet we have seen that the darkness hates the light we bring. Now the Vision of the Seven Trumpets tells us the only clear sound the world can hear each day is the sound of God's wrath and judgment. Worse than that, as we watch the people in darkness react to the trumpets' call, it is clear that they cannot understand the warning God is giving them. We can't help but wonder how unbelievers will ever find God's light under these conditions?

At this point we have to realize we have seen only half the picture of the Vision of the Seven Trumpets. God has shown us that the warning of his impending wrath and judgment will be prominently announced in this world. All people will hear it. Now God is going to show us the rest of the picture. In Revelation chapters ten and eleven God will reveal three new visions. These visions will complete the Vision of the Seven Trumpets of Judgment. In them God will make it clear that while the trumpets are loudly warning of his wrath in this world, God will be just as prominently proclaiming the message of his light for all to see and hear. Both messages, God's warning and God's light, will be clearly seen and heard by all until Jesus comes again.

Read Revelation 10:1-11

THE VISION OF THE MIGHTY ANGEL

After the sixth trumpet sounds revealing the terrible growing judgment of the Lord's wrath in the final days just before the end, John sees another angel coming down from heaven. This angel was visually impressive. He was *"robed in a cloud"* and had a *"rainbow above his head."* His face *"was like the sun"* and his legs *"were like fiery pillars."* But the most impressive part about him was his tremendous size. God calls our attention to this fact with the details he reveals in the vision. This angel was so large that all could see him. With one foot on the land and the other on the sea, and with a voice like the roar of a lion, when he spoke, all in the world could hear him.

That is the main point of the vision. This angel announces the Gospel Covenant for all the world to hear. Even as the Seven Trumpets of Judgment continue to blow with the warning of God's wrath, the Mighty Angel will be roaring the message of the Gospel, inviting sinners to find hope in the light of the Lord. Everyone in this world will hear that message as well. The Gospel message the angel proclaims is written on the *"little scroll"* which *"lay open in his hand."*

The two visions together, the Trumpets blowing and the Angel shouting, are still hard for Christians to reconcile. We can't help but feel that message of light would be more easily received and understood if it was not competing with the trumpet sounds. We wonder why both have to sound together. Against the backdrop of these concerns, John hears another sound as the Mighty Angel roars. The sound of the Gospel in the Mighty Angel's voice is confirmed by the Seven Thunders, a sound so loud it overcomes the trumpet sounds. That message we welcome in the vision. What happens next is surprising.

John hears the Seven Thunders sound their message confirming the voice of the Mighty Angel. John takes pen in hand at once to write down what the Seven Thunders say. God is revealing his message of light and hope and John wants to record every word. Just as he is about to write, a voice from heaven speaks commanding John not to write down what the Seven Thunders say. We will not learn what that message says until the Day of Judgment when Jesus returns.

This command from heaven addresses the discomfort we feel as we contrast the message of the Trumpets of Judgment with the message of the Mighty Angel. There is much we do not understand about what God is doing at this moment as he shines his light into a world that does not want it. With the sealing of the Seven Thunders, God is letting us know that there is much we will not know about how he carries out his plan in this world. He wants us to expect that there will be questions unanswered and actions unexplained. The ways of God are far above the ways of man and with the sealing of the Seven Thunders, God is stating that truth again. There is a time to understand what God is doing and there is a time to trust the Lord even when we do not understand. The sealed thunders remind us of this truth.

As John reacts to the command from heaven, the Mighty Angel speaks. *"There will be no more delay! ⁷ But in the days when the seventh angel is about to sound his trumpet, the mystery of God will be accomplished, just as he announced to his servants the prophets."* (Rev.

10:6,7 NIV) The holy God has a plan for this sinful world. He intends to make it possible for sinful people to be accepted before his holy throne. Paul referred to this mysterious plan. *And he made known to us the mystery of his will according to his good pleasure, which he purposed in Christ,* [10] *to be put into effect when the times will have reached their fulfillment—to bring all things in heaven and on earth together under one head, even Christ.* (Eph. 1:9,10 NIV) Now the time is rapidly approaching when the plan will be completed. The world can't afford to ignore the message of the Mighty Angel. God's victory over the forces of evil will be made known for all to see and hear on that day.

The urgency noted by the Mighty Angel now affects John and all the lampstands of the Lord. The angel gives John an unusual command. John is ordered to take the scroll from the angel's hand and then he is commanded to eat the scroll. John obeys. *I took the little scroll from the angel's hand and ate it.* (Rev. 10:10 NIV) This is something we have seen before in the Bible. The prophet Ezekiel had the very same experience when God in a vision commanded him to eat the scroll of God's word. Eating the scroll takes the word of God inside of the prophet. He is now filled with the word and able then to share that word with the world around him.

John describes the taste. *It tasted as sweet as honey in my mouth.* (Rev. 10:10a NIV) God's message of hope and light surely is welcomed and tastes good in the mouth of God's children. Psalm 19 tells us that God's words are *"... sweeter than honey; than honey from the comb."* That we understand. John goes on to say something that might surprise us. *"But when I had eaten it, my stomach turned sour."* (Rev. 10:10b NIV) While the message of hope is sweet to the taste, the experience of carrying that message into the world is not. The world will object to the message of the light and the world will reject and punish those who carry that light. Thus having the message of God will produce "indigestion" in our lives.

With that clearly understood, God gives John the command of the lampstands. *"You must prophesy again about many peoples, nations, languages and kings."* (Rev. 10:11 NIV) It does not matter that the darkness hates the light. It does not matter that the world opposes the message. These facts do not make the message any less necessary or any less vital for all people to hear. Therefore in the face of opposition God commands his people to carry this message into the world. Our work is that of the Mighty Angel and we are the voice of that angel in this world.

With this vision God refocuses our attention on the purpose for each new day in this world, a purpose God revealed with the Vision of Christ Among the Lampstands. God is reaching out to the whole world with his message of hope before it is too late. The Trumpets of Judgment blowing the news of God's wrath against unbelievers does not change that fact. So even as we hear the trumpets blow, God urges us to carry on the work of shining his light. The Vision of the Mighty Angel assures us that this work will not be in vain. The Gospel will be heard and in a world filled with despair, people will be able to find hope in the light God offers. *As the rain and the snow come down from heaven, and do not return to it without watering the earth and making it bud and flourish, so that it yields seed for the sower and bread for the eater, ¹¹so is my word that goes out from my mouth: It will not return to me empty, but will accomplish what I desire and achieve the purpose for which I sent it.* (Isaiah 55:10,11 NIV)

Read Revelation 11:1,2

THE VISION OF THE MEASURING ROD

Chapter eleven of the Revelation brings us to the conclusion of the Vision of the Seven Trumpets of Judgment. In this chapter God reveals two truths we need to know about the visible church of God. The first truth we find in the Vision of the Measuring Rod. John was given a measuring rod and was commanded to *"...measure the temple of*

God ... and count the worshipers there." Remember Jesus' comforting words in the Gospel of John? *My sheep listen to my voice; I know them, and they follow me. ²⁸ I give them eternal life, and they shall never perish; no one can snatch them out of my hand.* (John 10:27,28 NIV) The Vision of the Measuring Rod is a commentary on this verse, another example of the Bible explaining itself. By sending John to measure the temple and to count the worshipers, God is assuring believers that he is going to protect them in this world as they carry out the work of lampstands. Jesus is continually watching over his people in his church as they spread his light into the darkness.

But God goes on to show John and us a disquieting truth about the visible church in the second part of the vision. *But exclude the outer court; do not measure it, because it has been given to the Gentiles. They will trample on the holy city for 42 months.* (Rev. 11:2 NIV) While God is protecting his people in his church, God tells us that we will see the church overrun by the darkness until Jesus returns. Using the familiar image of the Temple in Jerusalem, God reveals that his visible church will be divided like the ancient temple into the *"inner court"* and the *"outer court."* The *"inner court"* is occupied by God's believing children, his lampstands eager to share the light of God. John measures the court and counts the believers, indicating that God knows his people by name and watches over them. The *"outer court"* of the visible church will be filled with people who do not belong to God. These unbelievers, *"gentiles"* as God calls them in the vision, will appear to the world to be part of the visible Christian church. However, they will offer "darkness" instead of "light" to the world, and they will do so in God's name. As a result, we will all see examples of God's visible church saying things God did not say and doing things God would not do. This will be true for *"42 months,"* the full time of the New Testament until Jesus returns. This is the new truth God teaches us about the visible church in the Vision of the Measuring Rod.

Reviewing the Meaning of the Number Three and One-Half

At this point it is important that we pause in our study to review the message God presents to us by his use of certain numbers in the Revelation. We already learned that God uses the number seven to represent his Gospel Covenant. Whenever God uses seven he wants us to keep in mind that he is actively reaching out to this world with his message of light through faith in Jesus and whatever he is currently showing us in a given vision plays a role in accomplishing that covenant.

God attaches an equally important reminder to the number three and one-half. This number occurs in different forms in the Revelation. It appears as *"times and time and half a time"* or *"42 months"* or *"1260 days"* or even simply *"3 1/2 days."* The important thing to see is that whenever God mentions this number, it is always in connection with some form of *"rebellion against God."* During the entire time of the New Testament there will be people living in rebellion against God. They will embrace the darkness and oppose the light. This fact leads us to conclude that the number three and one-half represents the "Broken Covenant" when it is used in the Revelation. God uses it to remind us why his judgments are necessary every day on this earth.

In the visions we find in Revelation chapter eleven, God uses this number to show us that we will see this rebellion even in his visible church. Unbelievers will overrun the visible church of God. The Two Witnesses will face the constant opposition of the world. Until Jesus comes again God reveals that we will see the unbelievers make God's churches places of darkness instead of light. In chapter twelve we will see Satan persecute the church of God for *"1260 days,"* the full New Testament period. In all these cases God is reminding us that the people of the Broken Covenant are actively opposing God.

When we remember this, we have a complete answer to all that we see in this world using a simple numerical formula. The algorithm has two components giving a complete spiritual explanation. Why is there so much evil in the world when God is holy and good? The answer is three and one-half! The world loves the darkness and people live in full rebellion against the Lord, forcing God to show them his wrath to warn them to repent. Why would God allow the world to continue if it is filled with rebellion? The answer is seven! God is reaching out with his covenant every day. That work is so important that God is willing to let this evil world exist another day on the premise that he can reach even one more soul. Keep these numbers in mind as you study the Revelation visions, and you will find comfort and clarity every step of the way.

The Lesson of the Vision of the Measuring Rod

Rebellion within the church of God as revealed by the Vision of the Measuring Rod should not come as a complete surprise to us. When he walked this earth Jesus warned us that false teachers would be present in the church. *Watch out for false prophets. They come to you in sheep's clothing, but inwardly they are ferocious wolves. 16 By their fruit you will recognize them. ... 17 Likewise every good tree bears good fruit, but a bad tree bears bad fruit. 18 A good tree cannot bear bad fruit, and a bad tree cannot bear good fruit. 19 Every tree that does not bear good fruit is cut down and thrown into the fire. 20 Thus, by their fruit you will recognize them. 21 "Not everyone who says to me, 'Lord, Lord,' will enter the kingdom of heaven, but only he who does the will of my Father who is in heaven. 22 Many will say to me on that day, 'Lord, Lord, did we not prophesy in your name, and in your name drive out demons and perform many miracles?' 23 Then I will tell them plainly, 'I never knew you. Away from me, you evildoers!'"* (Matt. 7:15-23 NIV) The Apostle Peter issued the same warning. *But there were also false prophets among the people, just as there will be false teachers among you. They will secretly introduce destructive heresies, even denying the sovereign Lord who bought them—bringing swift destruction on themselves. 2 Many will follow their shameful ways and will bring the way of truth into disrepute.* ³ *In their greed these teachers will exploit you with stories they have made up. Their condemnation has long been hanging over them, and their destruction has not been sleeping.* (2 Peter 2:1-3 NIV) The Apostle Paul warned that people would welcome false prophets into the church to preach messages that were more pleasing to them than the truth of God. Remember, we should expect to see people, even in the church, who love the darkness rather than the light. *For the time will come when men will not put up with sound doctrine. Instead, to suit their own desires, they will gather around them a great number of teachers to say what their itching ears want to hear.* (2 Tim. 4:3 NIV) The Vision of the Measuring Rod pictures this truth and explains what we see in the visible churches of our world.

Isaiah warned one day people would come into this world and offer darkness as if it was light. *Woe to those who call evil good and good evil, who put darkness for light and light for darkness, who put bitter for sweet and sweet for bitter.* (Isaiah 5:20 NIV) God reveals that this will happen within the walls of his church until Christ comes again. So it should come as no surprise that we will find churches today who claim to represent God and yet never mention the word "sin." After all, people of this world do not like that word or what it says about their lives. We will find churches today that embrace the most vile forms of perverted behavior in the name of "love" and "tolerance." These places of "false light" will declare that God welcomes such darkness into his presence with no reservations or demand for repentance. We will see churches today abandon the work of spreading the light of God's covenant through faith in Christ because they will find it more worthy to spend their energy righting the things they think are unjust in this world. We will see people standing within the walls of God's church saying and doing the most offensive things in God's eyes and then claiming to be following God. Until the Lord Jesus returns, we can expect to find such darkness within the walls of God's visible church. The *"gentiles"* will trample the courts of God for *"42 months."*

Read Revelation 11:3-14

THE VISION OF THE TWO WITNESSES

However horrifying this truth may be, God wants us to know that the presence of darkness so close to the center of God's temple will not hinder God's message from being preached in this world clearly for all to hear. God showed us that in the Vision of the Seven Letters and in the Vision of the Mighty Angel and through the *"inner court"* in the Vision of the Measuring Rod. Now he repeats that idea in the Vision of the Two Witnesses. *And I will give power to my two witnesses, and they will prophesy for 1,260 days, clothed in sackcloth.* (Rev. 11:3 NIV) The darkness that invades the church of God will not prevent the lampstands from accomplishing their mission. In spite of the darkness the church of God will continue to proclaim its light for all to see and to hear. God says here his *"two witnesses"* will prophesy for 1,260 days. Again we find the number three and one-half reminding us that God is dealing with a world where people live in the Broken Covenant, defying God with their open rebellion. This will be the reality in our world until Jesus returns.

Yet during this whole time God's Two Witnesses will continue to prophesy. The fact that God mentions "two" witnesses is rooted in the Old Testament mandate. *One witness is not enough to convict a man accused of any crime or offense he may have committed. A matter must be established by the testimony of two or three witnesses.* (Deut. 19:15 NIV) God assures us that the truth of his Gospel will be fully attested to for the entire New Testament time by Two Witnesses, so there will be no doubt about the veracity of their message. Their message will call the world to repent of its rebellion before it is too late. That is why John sees that the witnesses are dressed in "sackcloth," a way to show the world that they were walking a path of repentance and sorrow over sin.

John goes on to describe the witnesses with a picture from the Old Testament book of Zechariah. *These are the two olive trees and the two lampstands that stand before the Lord of the earth.* (Rev. 11:4 NIV) Zechariah, the prophet, saw a vision of a lampstand burning in the Temple. Alongside the lampstand were two live olive trees supplying the lampstand continuously with oil. God was telling Zechariah that the light of the lamp would continue to burn because it was fed oil from the living olive trees. That is the idea God conveys in the vision John saw. God tells us that the Two Witnesses are like the living olive trees, supplied with a continuous message from God and delivering that message without interruption to the world for the entire period of time in question.

The world will not welcome the message. Darkness hates the light. But God assured John that his Two Witnesses would be equipped to stand against the rebellious world. *If anyone tries to harm them, fire comes from their mouths and devours their enemies. This is how anyone who wants to harm them must die. ⁶ These men have power to shut up the sky so that it will not rain during the time they are prophesying; and they have power to turn the waters into blood and to strike the earth with every kind of plague as often as they want.* (Rev. 11:5,6 NIV) God uses imagery here that reminds us of how the prophet Elijah stood against wicked King Ahab and his evil Queen Jezebel, commanding the heavens not to rain for over three years as a sign of God's wrath. God reminds us of the day when Moses and Aaron stood against the evil pharaoh and afflicted the land of Egypt with ten punishing plagues. That is the power God will give his witnesses to stand against the world's objection.

Such will be the case until the very last days, the days we know as *"Satan's little season."* Here the Lord reveals something new, something not told us before in the Bible. *Now when they have finished their testimony, the beast that comes up from the Abyss will attack them, and overpower and kill them. ⁸ Their bodies will lie in the street of the great city, which is figuratively called Sodom and Egypt, where also their Lord was crucified. ⁹ For three and a half days men from every people, tribe, language and nation will gaze on their bodies* *and refuse them burial. ¹⁰ The inhabitants of the earth will gloat over them and will celebrate by sending each other gifts, because these two prophets had tormented those who live on the earth.* (Rev. 11:7-10 NIV) Jesus reveals that in the last days just before he returns it will appear as if evil will triumph once and for all over the light of God. In this vision we see Satan killing God's Two Witnesses. The people of the world will celebrate the deaths of the Two Witnesses because now the tormenting truth of the light which was so troubling to the darkness will appear to be defeated.

And then, when the forces of darkness are sure the light has been defeated once and for all, a miracle will occur. *But after the three and a half days a breath of life from God entered them, and they stood on their feet, and terror struck those who saw them. ¹² Then they heard a loud voice from heaven saying to them, "Come up here." And they went up to heaven in a cloud, while their enemies looked on. ¹³ At that very hour there was a severe earthquake and a tenth of the city collapsed. Seven thousand people were killed in the earthquake, and the survivors were terrified and gave glory to the God of heaven. ¹⁴ The second woe has passed; the third woe is coming soon.* (Rev. 11:11-14 NIV) God will raise the witnesses to life and the wrath of God will be even more apparent to the world. When it seems that all the people of God are gone and there is no one left, suddenly the lampstands of the Lord will appear again out of nowhere. This pictures the spiritual chaos on this earth as the world passes through its final days.

God's point in the Vision of the Two Witnesses is to assure his people that his message will continue to be present even in the face of great opposition. This is true even though God's visible church will be overrun by people of the Broken Covenant. This will be true even in the final terrible days when evil will seem to have won. So as we shine God's light into the world and face the opposition of the darkness, God encourages us not to lose heart. Instead, listen every day for the sound of the Seventh Trumpet.

Read Revelation 11:15-19

THE SEVENTH TRUMPET

This is how God ends the Vision of the Seven Trumpets of Judgment. *The seventh angel sounded his trumpet, and there were loud voices in heaven, which said: "The kingdom of the world has become the kingdom of our Lord and of his Christ, and he will reign forever and ever."* (Rev. 11:15 NIV) The victory of the Lord will be revealed on the day he returns to this earth. Heaven will be filled with cries that define the victory, noting that the Lord will now reign forever. It is fitting that this vision ends with the full church of God in heaven. The 24 elders, the Old and New Testament Church of God, fall before the Lord in thanks and praise to God for what he has done. They thank God for the victory he has won. They eagerly celebrate that now it is time for reward to God's own and judgment for those who opposed the Lord. John sees the glory of God revealed as heaven opens before him. *Then God's temple in heaven was opened, and within his temple was seen the ark of his covenant. And there came flashes of lightning, rumblings, peals of thunder, an earthquake and a great hailstorm.* (Rev. 11:19 NIV)

Chapter Summary

The Vision of the Seven Trumpets of Judgment carries a frightening and sobering message of God's wrath. The judgments of God will be so prominent in this world every day that all people will see them. However, this is only half the message God wants his lampstands to see. God records the visions in Revelation chapters ten and eleven to complete the picture of what we can expect to see in this world until Jesus returns. During this time the Trumpets will blow each day, warning of God's judgment. But at the same time, the Mighty Angel and the Two Witnesses will be proclaiming the Gospel of God just as prominently, inviting people to embrace the hope God offers through faith in Christ. Taken together, the warning in the Vision of the Seven Trumpets of Judgment will be balanced in this world by the equally visible and prominent message of the Gospel Covenant.

The Vision of the Mighty Angel *addresses our concern regarding the prominence of the Trumpets of Judgment. The Trumpets are so loud that everyone in the world will hear them. To us it seems that the trumpet sounds will drown out the Gospel sound and make it that much harder to reach people with the message of God's grace. God speaks to that concern with the Vision of the Mighty Angel. This Angel is so large and speaks so loudly that everyone can hear him. He will be present for the entire period of time from the first to the second coming of Jesus. He announces the Gospel message of God. With this vision God is assuring us that while the Trumpets of Judgment are sounding the warning of God's impending wrath, the Mighty Angel will be just as clearly heard announcing the message of God's grace in Christ. The people of this world will hear both messages until Jesus returns.*

The Vision of the Measuring Rod *carries the discussion of the Gospel presence in this world further. In this vision God reveals a truth about the visible Christian Church. God tells us that we will see the darkness overrun the visible church and it will possess the "outer courts." Therefore we will hear the church that represents God say things God would never say and do things God would never do. However, God wants us to see that even in times of terrible betrayal, God has counted the "inner court" of the church, and they will continue to faithfully carry on God's work of light sharing until Jesus returns.*

The Vision of the Two Witnesses *helps to balance the message of the Vision of the Trumpets as well, just like the Vision of the Mighty Angel. The Two Witnesses carry a message of repentance and hope into the world while the Trumpets are blowing. Though the world will not appreciate the message, God will protect the witnesses and empower them to do their job until shortly before Jesus returns. Note that there are "two" witnesses which assures us that the message of God's grace and hope through faith in Christ will be clearly presented and be beyond question in this world, even while the Trumpets of Judgment are blowing.*

CHAPTER TEN
The Vision of the Seven Visions:
Part One

Revelation Chapters 12 & 13

Introduction

We live in a world which is increasingly technologically advanced. The more things advance, the more complicated things become. The more complicated things become, the more we are willing to settle for understanding the "what" of things even if we don't fully understand the "why" of things. Sometimes we just don't need to know why things happen. For example, most of us have become very comfortable operating a moving vehicle with only a minimum of knowledge. As long as we know where to put the fuel and where to insert the key, we are fine with not understanding how an internal combustion engine operates. The "why" is less important than the "what" in our lives in an increasing number of instances.

However, that is not true when it comes to understanding the world around us. In the first eleven chapters of the Revelation, God has shown us "what" will happen in this world. God revealed, that until Jesus returns again, the world will be in turmoil. There will be wars and famines and disease and persecution of Christians and death. These events will make suffering and loss common to the experience of every human being. After reading these chapters, we know "what" will happen. But God wants us to know more than this. God wants us to also understand "why" these things are happening. Right now we know the Red Horse of war and the Black Horse of economic hardship will ride in everyone's life, but we do not know why they ride. This is what God intends to show us in the next vision, the Vision of the Seven Visions.

This vision is recorded in chapters twelve to fifteen of Revelation. God is going to show us seven individual pictures. They will reveal what is happening beneath the surface of what we see in this world. The visions are connected to each other by the introductory words in Greek, *"and I saw..."* We will cover these in two chapters beginning with this one in which we will study Revelation chapters twelve and thirteen.

Read Revelation 12:1-13

THE VISION OF THE WOMAN, THE DRAGON AND THE CHILD

God begins our education in the "why" of this world by taking us back in time to the moment it all began. In the first of the Seven Visions we see the Vision of the Woman and the Dragon. Here God presents three characters which serve as pictures or metaphors. The imagery in the vision is so familiar that most Christians will need no guidance in identifying the historical moment God is describing. Remembering that God says what he means and he means what he says, we will trust God himself to explain what he is teaching us in this vision.

First God introduces us to the Woman. John describes her in detail. She was *"clothed with the sun."* She had the *"moon under her feet."* She wore a *"crown of twelve stars"* on her head, and most remarkable of all, *"she was pregnant and .... about to give birth."* The first question we face is, "Who is this woman?" Some Christians in the Roman Catholic Church at once assume that the woman is a picture of Mary, the mother of Jesus. They reason that if the child to be born is Jesus, and it clearly was, then the woman must be Mary. However, the words God wrote show us this conclusion is too narrow. The woman in the vision gives birth to the child and then she is carried off into the wilderness where God keeps her safe *"for 1,260 days."* That time period represents the entire time of the New Testament. Therefore this "woman" cannot be just one human being.

Her identity lies in two specific details in the vision. First, she wears a *"crown with twelve stars,"* twelve, the number of the church of God. Wherever God uses that number in the Revelation he is either making a promise to his church, or as in this case, he is keeping a promise to his church. The fact that there are 12 stars here and not 24 as in other places shows us that we are dealing with the church of God in the Old Testament. The second thing to notice about the woman is that *"she was pregnant ... and about to give birth."* The Old Testament church carried the promise of a Savior through the centuries. The woman in this picture is the church of God pregnant with the promise of a Savior.

However, the vision reveals that there was someone else awaiting the moment of this birth. John sees *"... an enormous red dragon with seven heads and ten horns and seven crowns on his heads."* (Rev. 12:3 NIV) God tells us that this dragon is Satan himself. He is a fearsome creature who covers himself with the number seven, the covenant number, attempting to mask who he is. But something is off. While he has seven heads and wears seven crowns like the Lamb we saw earlier, he has ten horns. The vision reveals two terrifying details about this dragon. First, he is not alone. He swept a third of the stars from heaven with his mighty tail. Most likely this is a reference to the rebellion the devil led in heaven against God at the dawn of time and the many angels who followed his lead. Second, his intent is pure evil. He wants to destroy the child to whom the woman gives birth as soon as the child is born.

She gave birth to a son, a male child, who will rule all the nations with an iron scepter. (Rev. 12:5 NIV) This child is the Christ. He is the king God had promised from David's line. His rule will be absolute, *"with an iron scepter."* None can resist it. The devil wanted to destroy this child. We know from the Bible how the devil incited King Herod to slaughter the babies in Bethlehem in an attempt to kill this special child. God warned Joseph to flee to Egypt to save the child from that moment. The devil continued his attempts to destroy the Savior throughout Jesus' walk on this earth, right up to the moment of the cross on Calvary. And we know that in that moment, what appeared to be a final victory for Satan, was actually a victory for the Lord. As John puts it, *"... her child was snatched up to God and to his throne."* (Rev. 12:5 NIV) God kept the child safe and brought him to his throne in heaven.

When that happened, the Dragon turned his rage on the woman. *The woman fled into the desert to a place prepared for her by God, where she might be taken care of for 1,260 days.* (Rev. 12:6 NIV) Again we see God measure the time of the New Testament with the number of the Broken Covenant. During this time as the Dragon tried to harm God's church, God kept her safe in the wilderness, much as he protected Israel through 40 years of wandering in the Sinai wilderness.

God goes on in the vision to give us a closer look at what was happening behind the scene in this spiritual war. *"And there was war in heaven..."* What a jarring scene, war in heaven! The angels of God battled with the forces of Satan and defeated them. *But he was not strong enough, and they lost their place in heaven.* [9] *The great dragon was hurled down—that ancient serpent called the devil, or Satan, who leads the whole world astray. He was hurled to the earth, and his angels with him.* (Rev. 12:8 NIV) The dominant question in our minds as we watch this battle take place is the question "when." When did this battle occur?

We find the answer in the words that the beings of heaven sang as they rejoiced in the victory. *"The accuser of our brothers ... has been hurled down."* Satan was defeated and hurled to the earth. It was *"the blood of the Lamb"* that overcame Satan. With these words God makes it plain that he is describing what happened behind the scene as Jesus carried out the plan of salvation on this earth. The deciding moment came when Christ shed his blood for all mankind on the cross. With that act Satan was once and for all defeated. No longer can Satan stand in the halls of heaven and accuse the children of God as he did with ancient Job and Zechariah. Now the blood of Jesus exonerates the people of this earth completely. Heaven bursts forth with great joy and celebration. Satan is banished along with his evil followers.

Yet, as good as this news is, there is a cost to this earth. *But woe to the earth and the sea, because the devil has gone down to you! He is filled with fury, because he knows that his time is short.* (Rev. 12:11 NIV) This simple verse explains all that we see on this earth. This is the "why" God wants us to understand about all that we see. The violence, the murders, the wars, the diseases and suffering --- none of this is random. None of this is accidental. The Vision of the Woman and the Dragon reveals that behind all the pain and all the suffering and all the loss is the rage of an angry Red Dragon. He knows he has been defeated. He knows Christ is coming again. He knows his time is short. Now this Dragon is focused on pouring out his rage on every inhabitant of this earth for as long as he can.

It is this Dragon and his rage that bring suffering and pain and loss into our lives. It is this Dragon who incites sinful people to rebel against God and his covenant, and by that rebellion to bring the judgment of God into their lives. It is this Dragon who attacks our relationship with God and, in every way he can, tries to weaken our trust in the love this God has demonstrated for us in his son. *For our struggle is not against flesh and blood, but against the rulers, against the authorities, against the powers of this dark world and against the spiritual forces of evil in the heavenly realms.* (Eph. 6:12,13 NIV) Woe indeed to all who walk this earth in the face of this rage.

God goes on to explain how the devil will carry out his rage. Satan first turned his full attention to the church of God, trying to destroy the church as he had hoped to destroy the child. We see this in the vision as the Dragon pursues the Woman in the wilderness, trying to destroy her. Using mighty and seemingly overwhelming power, the devil turned his full fury against the church. Yet in the moments when it seemed he would succeed, God time and again rescued the church and kept her safe. God gave her *"wings of an eagle"* when needed and had the earth *"swallow the raging flood"* which came from the Dragon.

While God does not cite specific historical events with this vision, the history of the devil's assault on the church after Jesus ascended into heaven can be seen in many ways in the New Testament. As soon as Jesus ascended the devil incited the Jews to persecute the Christians with a vengeance, forcing the Christians to scatter across the world seeking safety. History shows how the devil used the Roman government to continue the persecution trying to destroy the church. Yet the more the persecution continued, the more the church seemed to grow and prosper. Even though the powers of opposition to the church were clearly stronger, God miraculously kept his church alive, keeping Jesus' promise that *"the gates of hell will not prevail"* against her.

When it became clear that God would not allow the devil to destroy the church, the devil turned his attention to the individual people of the church, the woman's *"offspring."* This is the "why" each Christian faces. There is a Dragon who stalks our path. Using powerful lies and constant delusion, he promises us happiness and then fills our lives with misery. He fills our lives with pain and suffering and then rejoices in the pain he causes. The presence of this angry Red Dragon in our lives assures us of one certainty until Jesus comes again. We will face spiritual war every day as this savage enemy attacks our relationship with God. His goal is to tear us from the hand of God. This spiritual war in our lives and in the lives of all people is the reason for the darkness we see everywhere we look in this world. This is the warning of which God wants us to take note as we begin each day of our lives. *But woe to the earth and the sea, because the devil has gone down to you! He is filled with fury, because he knows that his time is short.* (Rev. 12:11 NIV)

Read Revelation 13:1-10

THE VISION OF THE BEAST OF THE SEA

In Revelation chapter thirteen God continues to reveal why things happen on this earth as they do. God reveals two new enemies which will join the Dragon's efforts to harm the people of God. John sees the first of those enemies emerge from the sea. This enemy resembled the Dragon himself with *"ten horns"* and *"seven heads"* and *"ten crowns."* He opposed God having *"a blasphemous name"* written on each head. Remember as we read any part of the Bible, our first step is always to look closely at the words God writes. God says what he means and he means what he says. So as God reveals this strange and frightening creature, we expect that God will explain his meaning with his own words. In this case God's description of the Beast of the Sea clearly identifies this creature's major characteristic. This beast possesses *"governing authority"* which he exercises *"... over every tribe, people, language and nation"* on this earth until Jesus comes again. God uses the number *"42 months"* to show us this and at the same time to remind us that this is another example of the rebellion that will be opposing God in this world until Jesus returns.

Notice that this beast comes out of the sea. The Dragon did not create the beast. God did. Romans 13 makes it clear that God alone creates ruling authority and gives it power. *There is no authority except that which God has established. The authorities that exist have been established by God.* (Rom. 13:1 NIV) The fact that this beast rules over all the people of the earth for the entire time until Jesus returns reveals that this beast is a picture of the governments of this world. When the Dragon was not able to destroy the church with his immense power, the Dragon saw in the Beast of the Sea another option. God is revealing that the Dragon will subvert governments to do his bidding and the Dragon will then give this beast his tremendous power to use against God, his Gospel Covenant, and God's people who carry God's light. *He was given power to make war against the saints and to conquer them.* (Rev. 13:7 NIV) So in this vision God reveals that we will see the devil use governments in this world to oppose God and his covenant. The Beast of the Sea is a political beast, *"anti-Christian government"* in all its forms.

As we look elsewhere in the Bible, we find support for this understanding that this Beast of the Sea represents anti-Christian government. In chapter seven of the book of Daniel, the prophet reports that God gave him a vision of this beast in a dream. In his dream Daniel saw four beasts come up *"out of the sea,"* the same place from which the beast in the Revelation came. While Daniel saw four beasts, the descriptions of each beast were the same as the description of the beast in the Revelation. Daniel said these beasts resembled a lion, a bear and a leopard, and the fourth beast had ten horns. John describes the Beast of the Sea with similar words. *The beast I saw resembled a leopard, but had feet like those of a bear and a mouth like that of a lion.* (Rev. 13:2 NIV)

In Daniel, God goes on to identify this beast. *The four great beasts are four kingdoms that will rise from the earth.* (Dan. 7:17 NIV) God told Daniel that the four beasts that came from the sea in his dream were four governments that were yet to come. Supported by God's association of the beasts in Daniel with governments, we gain more confidence in concluding that this Beast of the Sea in the Revelation is a picture of ruling governments in this world. These governments will join the Dragon in opposing God's church and his people. The anti-Christian governments will be so strong that in the eyes of the people of the world, none will be able to oppose it or to resist its power. *Men worshiped the dragon because he had given authority to the beast, and they also worshiped the beast and asked, "Who is like the beast? Who can make war against him?"* (Rev. 13:4 NIV)

One puzzling piece of the Revelation is left unexplained. John reports what he calls a *"fatal wound"* to one of the heads of the Beast of the Sea. The "mortal wound" seems to represent some sort of reversal suffered by this beast preventing it from carrying out its intention to serve the wishes of the Dragon by attacking the church. This reversal seemed like it might be a permanent change, but then to the amazement of the world, it came back to life again. The simplest understanding of this image may be that there will be times when a government in this world temporarily abandons its opposition to God and his churches.

There have been historical moments when this seemed to occur. Some point to Emperor Constantine's conversion. At that time the government reversed its position. Instead of using its power to oppose the church, led by the emperor Constantine who was recently converted, the government ceased its persecution of the church. This change proved to be only a temporary phenomenon. It did not take many years for the government to resume its anti-Christian path. We can expect that until Jesus comes again, we will continue to see moments like this. Perhaps the temporary seemingly *"fatal wound"* suffered by one of the heads on the beast pictures these moments.

As with all things in the Revelation, when an unexplained sign like this occurs within one of God's visions, there are many people willing to offer a guess as to its meaning. In the end, no matter how rational the arguments supporting the guesses may be, without clear statements from God himself, they remain only guesses. For our purposes we will leave the meaning of the *"fatal wound"* to the last day when the Lord himself will reveal it to us.

God describes the impressive governing power and the strong opposition of this beast to the church of God. In Daniel's dream God revealed that the beast he saw represented earthly governments. From this we can conclude that this Beast of the Sea is a "political beast" who uses its power to oppose God and his people. Some Bible students have tried to identify this beast as a specific government in history. For example, many Lutheran commentators from the era of the Reformation identified this beast as the Roman government in the days of the early church. While the Roman government surely was one iteration of the Beast of the Sea, we must remember that the metaphors of each vision in the Revelation reveal truths which will apply to the full time period between the first and the second coming of Jesus. For this reason we must assume God is not identifying just one anti-Christian government with this vision. Rather he is picturing all governments.

Christians in every age will see this Beast of the Sea and he will bring hardship into the lives of the people of God. It will not matter what form of government the beast may take. Whether a monarchy, a dictatorship, a communist government, or even a democratic government like America, the operating truth will be that the beast will *"blaspheme"* God, speaking against his truth and those who dare to stand with the Lord.

Those of us in America at this time who study the Revelation can find the Beast of the Sea residing in our own halls of government. In a country whose constitution was written to guarantee freedom to express our religion without government interference, we watch in amazement as people now use that same constitution to enforce a freedom from religion in America, using the government to suppress any public expression of allegiance to God. In a country founded by people who rejoiced in a firm belief in the care and guidance of their God, we find it is now against the law for our schools to even suggest that there is a God who created us, let alone cares for us. Elected leaders even go so far as to ridicule those who dare to believe the Bible when it reveals that God created the universe and gave us our lives. Here in America the Beast of the Sea brands the confession of God's truth as revealed in the Bible as "hate speech." If a Christian stands opposed to abortion on demand or to the perversion of homosexuality, the government leaders attack those words as "hate speech" and they go on to condemn the Christian who dared to quote God as being "divisive and intolerant." The Beast of the Sea walks among us and he will bring great harm to the lives of God's people.

It is this fact that causes the Lord to conclude this segment of the vision with a warning. *He who has an ear, let him hear. ¹⁰If anyone is to go into captivity, into captivity he will go. If anyone is to be killed with the sword, with the sword he will be killed.* (Rev. 13:9-10 NIV) This beast will walk the earth in every age until the Lord comes again. He will cause God's people much hardship. Some of God's people will be imprisoned by the beast and some will be killed, but God encourages us to face these conditions with *"patient endurance and faithfulness,"* trusting God to know and to do what is best for us. God has seen what the Dragon and the beast will do and God has included even these terrible things into his plan for our good.

Read Revelation 13:11-18

THE VISION OF THE BEAST OF THE EARTH

With that dire warning in place, John sees a second beast arise, this time from the earth. God describes this beast with two conflicting statements. This Beast of the Earth has *"two horns like a lamb."* While the Beast of the Sea in appearance was a very clear danger, this Beast of the Earth appears to be harmless. Even more than that, this beast appears to be on the side of the Lamb. To the world, the Beast of the Earth will look like "church." But when he opens his mouth, the beast will reveal his true character. John tells us this beast *"spoke like a dragon."* The message he offers supports the Dragon and opposes the truth of God. He uses his inside position to attack God and the people who follow him. This Beast of the Earth is a "religious beast" that opposes God and his message. The Beast of the Earth is *"anti-Christian religion,"* religion that claims to be of God and yet presents a message which is opposed to God and his people.

Later in the Revelation God confirms the identity of this beast as "religious" in character by giving him the title of the *"false prophet,"* one who claims to speak for God but who then delivers a message that is against God. God says that the Beast of the Earth will use his lies in God's name to deceive people on this earth, tricking them into following the Dragon and the Beast of the Sea. In the end God will punish this Beast of the Earth for his lies, along with all the other enemies of God.

The Beast of the Earth will use his lies to trick people into accepting the values and actions and priorities of the Beast of the Sea as honorable and noble. Just as the Beast of the Sea was given power by the Dragon, this second beast administers this same power from this same source for the same goal. He uses his power to perform signs that accompany his message. In this way he is able to deceive people on this earth and convince them to follow the Beast of the Sea. When the False Prophet succeeds in deceiving people, he places his mark upon them. Those who have the mark of the beast he rewards as they walk through this world. Those who do not bear the mark of the beast, the followers of the Lamb, he persecutes and kills.

God closes this vision by focusing our attention on the mark of this beast. *This calls for wisdom. If anyone has insight, let him calculate the number of the beast, for it is man's number. His number is 666.* (Rev. 13:18 NIV) Much has been written about this number. Many have supplied guesses as to its meaning. For us, the number and its mysterious meaning is simpler than we might at first suspect. Note that the number is 6 repeating. Add to this the character and essence of the Beast of the Earth. He tries to convince the world that he is of the Lamb, but all the while he speaks for the Dragon. If we combine those two thoughts we have a number. It strives with all its might to appear to the world to be the number seven, the number of the covenant, but it continually falls short. No matter how hard it tries, the best it can do is come close. Striving to appear as seven, the number achieves only 666 repeating.

What God is describing with this number is the clearest attribute of those who side with the Beast of the Earth and who follow his voice. In all they do, no matter how terrible, they will try to cover what they do with the appearance of the Lamb and his number seven. Like the Pharisees in Jesus' day who covered their sinful hearts with outward actions that appeared dedicated to serving God, so those who bear the mark of the beast will cover even their most ugly and offensive actions with a veneer of honorable intent. For example, defenders of abortion will speak in noble terms about a woman's right to control her own reproductive system. Defenders of homosexual marriage will speak in moral terms about justice and equality, civil rights and tolerance. In this world those who stand with the beast are praised for their compassion and their tolerance, and those who stand with the Lamb are condemned as evil and judgmental. So it will be until the Lord comes again.

With the visions of the two beasts, the stage is now set. We face three savage powerful enemies every day. This is the world in which we live. There is a Dragon filled with fury who rages against the people of this earth and especially against the people of God. This Dragon has two beasts that help him attack God's people. One is a political beast that uses the power of government to attack and oppose the church. The other is a religious beast that deceives people into thinking that anti-Christian governments are noble and right. This unholy trinity of enemies will cause much pain to the people of this earth. But through it all the Christian can be patient and endure. The Lord has seen this coming and incorporated these evil things into his plan. We can trust the Lord to watch over us in the face of these raging beasts and know that all is well. This is the message God gives in the remaining visions of the Seven Visions.

Chapter Summary

The Fifth Essential Revelation Truth

The hardship and suffering we see in this world are caused by an angry Red Dragon who, along with his helpers, is fighting a spiritual war against God and his followers. This is the reason why things happen as they do in this world.

The purpose of the Vision of the Seven Visions is to reveal the answer to the question "why." God has told us "what" will happen in the first eleven chapters of the Revelation. Now he explains "why" these things must happen.

We live in the midst of a huge spiritual war. Satan pours out his fury on the inhabitants of this world as he rages against the reality that *"his time is short."* This Red Dragon is the cause of the senseless evil and disasters that we see. This Dragon has two strong helpers in the form of anti-Christian government and anti-Christian religion. Together these three enemies bring misery and suffering to the lives of God's people and to the people of this world. No wonder God warned the world about the *"woe"* we would suffer until the Lord returns.

CHAPTER ELEVEN
The Vision of the Seven Visions: Part Two

Revelation Chapters 14 & 15

Introduction

In the Visions of the Seven Letters, the Seven Seals, the Seven Trumpets, the Mighty Angels, the Measuring of the Temple and the Two Witnesses, God has made it very clear "what" would happen in this world until Jesus returns. The Vision of the Seven Visions begins to explain "why" these things will happen. In the first three visions God reveals that the terrible things that happen in this world are the work of an angry Red Dragon and his two powerful helpers, the Beast of the Sea and the Beast of the Earth. These three mighty enemies bring pain and suffering to the lives of all people in this world.

That is what we have seen so far and the news is unsettling. It is disconcerting to know that an angry Red Dragon is stalking our lives eager to bring us pain and suffering. It is disconcerting to know that this Dragon will turn the forces of government and religion against us in his effort to harm us. These forces are much stronger than we are. Such news is sobering because it makes us wonder how we will ever survive with such powerful enemies as these.

Our natural reaction to this sobering news forms the foundation on which God builds the final four visions. We have three powerful enemies, but we are not alone in this world. We have a God who has secured our lives with his promises. This God has placed his mark on us and he watches over us every step of the way. God wants us to be aware of these spiritual enemies who lie under the surface of our life experience and who cause so much pain. We live in a physical world and we face physical challenges and trials. In reality, we are living our lives on the front lines of a spiritual war. Enemies much stronger than we are stand opposed to us and these enemies bring sorrow into our lives. But God wants us to live each day with hope and confidence, knowing all is well, even in the face of such foes. In the next four visions God will complete the picture of the Vision of Seven Visions showing us that we can be confident each day, secure in the promises of the Lord.

Read Revelation 14:1-5

THE VISION OF THE LAMB AND THE 144,000

The first vision John records in Revelation fourteen is called the Vision of the Lamb and the 144,000. As we examine this picture, the first thing we notice is the location where the vision takes place. The location is Mt. Zion, a metaphor for heaven. Long ago God made a promise to his people. *I have installed my King on Zion, my holy hill.* (Psalm 2:6 NIV) This vision pictures the day when God fulfills that promise. There we find the Lamb of God, and he is a welcomed sight after seeing the Beast of the Earth trying to deceive the world by impersonating the Lamb. The second thing we notice as we examine the vision is the participants. Here with the Lamb at the end of time we find the 144,000 people of God standing in fullness of joy in his presence.

We have met this group before. Remember that twelve is the number of the church. Wherever God uses this number in the Revelation he is either making a promise to his church or he is keeping a promise to his church. In this case it is the latter. The 144,000 with the Lord on Mt. Zion is a picture of God's full and complete church in heaven safe and secure from the Dragon and the beasts that meant them harm.

The fact that 144 (12 squared) and 1000 (the number 10 cubed) are combined indicates that this is the full church of God. No one is left behind. No one is lost.

The activity of this group in the vision confirms the location and the moment. We are witnessing a celebration. John compares the sound of the celebration to *"rushing waters"* and *"peals of thunder."* Yet it was not a frightening sound. John says it was the sound of *"harpists playing their harps."* The cause of the celebration lies in the song that they were playing. John calls it a *"new song."* It was a song never sung before. More than that, it was a song only they could sing.

The group pictured as the 144,000 were the people of God. They had been saved by the Lamb from these enemies and from the curse of sin into which they were born. These are people who had been born *"darkness"* but now by God's grace they were *"light in the Lord."* That light of God's grace they reflected in their lives as they walked the narrow path of the Lord in a world that preferred the broad road to hell. They lived a *"life of faith"* as they walked this earth and that life taught them the celebration song they sang in heaven in the presence of the Lamb.

John highlights three characteristics of the life God's grace equipped them to live. They *"did not defile themselves with women."* This is a metaphor. The Bible often uses the images of fornication or adultery to picture unfaithfulness to God. In the same way here God uses the picture of virginity to picture faithfulness to God. The people singing this new song lived lives faithful to the Lord when they walked this earth. The next picture confirms that idea. They *"followed the Lamb"* and guided their steps by his word. They lived by God's truth and avoided the devil's lies. While the Beast of the Earth filled the world with the lies of the Dragon, deceiving the unbelievers every day, these followers of the Lamb avoided the lies. They were not deceived by these lies and they did not speak these lies to others.

With this vision God makes sure we have a complete picture of what is happening in this world. We know "what" is happening and we know "why" it is happening. But the "what" and the "why" do us no good unless we view them in the proper context. We need to live each day with the same knowledge and context that the Dragon lives, the awareness that *"his time is short."* The 144,000 and the Lamb standing on Mt. Zion, which is another name for heaven, bring that full message into clear view. God calls us to live each day with Mt. Zion in sight. This sight is the key to living each day in *"patient endurance and faithfulness to the Lord."*

Read Revelation 14:6-13

THE VISION OF THE THREE ANGELS

In the Vision of the Three Angels God confronts another misconception that we might reach if we see only the Dragon and the two beasts raging in a seemingly unchecked way against the children of God. The enemies seem so powerful that none can stand against them. We wonder if "evil" will triumph. To that question God speaks as he gives John the next vision, the Vision of the Three Angels.

John sees an angel flying in *"midair."* Remember, each vision reveals a truth which all people will see until Jesus comes again. Everyone will see and hear this angel. The angel carries a message for the earth. John tells us the message is *"the eternal Gospel,"* the good news of God's sure and certain favor for all people through faith in Christ. This message will be visibly present on this earth for all to see no matter what the Dragon and the beasts may do. It might appear that evil is in control. It might seem like nothing can stand against such power. But no matter how dark it might seem, no matter how much visible damage the enemy may cause, God's light will always be visible. Hearts filled with despair will find a message that gives hope for each new day. That hope is the Gospel. This message is for all people in every nation. The angel calls to the earth in the shadow of this Gospel. *He said in a loud voice, "Fear God and give him glory, because the hour of his judgment has come."* (Rev. 14:7 NIV)

God is in control and the victory is his. The Beast of the Earth will use signs and wonders to move people to follow the Beast of the Sea. The people of the world will be amazed at the immense power of the Beast of the Sea. Together these beasts will lead the world to follow the Dragon. All that will happen. But the Lord will not stand silently by. God wants all people to be saved. Therefore even as the beasts are raging in this world, God will be announcing his message of hope and a future for all to hear. In a world where evil will be so prominent and prevalent, God's message of hope and life through faith in Christ will always be present until Jesus returns. The angel flying in midair will be seen and heard by every person.

God sends the second angel to reveal what he has planned for the Dragon and the beasts who help him. The power of the Dragon and his two beast helpers seems overwhelming. In the shadow of the pain and suffering they inflict on the earth, the second angel of God announces that God's enemies will be defeated! *"Fallen! Fallen is Babylon the Great."* (Rev. 14:8 NIV) In the Old Testament the nation of Babylon under Nebuchadnezzar conquered the city of Jerusalem and destroyed it. From that time on Babylon became a symbol of all the enemies of the people of God, the seat of evil. Using that image now God combines all the enemies that threaten the people of God in this world and he announces the certain future that awaits them. Babylon will fall. That is certain. Evil will not triumph.

The third angel adds to that thought. God issues a warning to all who dare to follow the beast upon this earth. Just as the enemies of the church of God will fall, so it will be for all those who followed those enemies. As we watch the False Prophet deceive so many, we might conclude in this world that the "smart play" is to follow his voice and to *"receive his mark."* After all, those who bear the mark of the beast will escape economic persecution. So following the beast seems like the easiest road to travel through life, the road most promising success. Those who do not listen to his temptations face economic hardship and even loss of life. Here God shows the future of those who bear the mark of the beast in the message of the third angel. There will be *"no rest"* for those who bear the *"mark"* of the beast. Those who stand with the beast will face the certain wrath of God. Great will be their torment and it will never end.

The Lord issues two final messages of comfort to his people as they walk through this dangerous world. First the Lord urges his people to trust him and to be patient. *This calls for patient endurance on the part of the saints who obey God's commandments and remain faithful to Jesus.* (Rev. 14:12 NIV) God calls upon us to be patient in the face of these raging enemies. He urges us to trust his promises. We can walk calmly through this dangerous world, even as the enemies of God and his people rage. Their time is short. The Lord has assured us of victory.

In this context the Lord offers the most surprising and comforting message of all. It speaks to the heart of any Christian who has stood in a cemetery to say goodbye to a loved one who died in the Lord. It offers comfort to any who have suffered loss at the hands of the Beast of the Sea or the Beast of the Earth or the Dragon himself. What appears to be loss is actually gain for the child of God. Listen to the promise of God. *Then I heard a voice from heaven say, "Write: Blessed are the dead who die in the Lord from now on."* (Rev. 14:13 NIV) The cemeteries we visit may seem permanent. But God tells his people not to believe their eyes. The Lord has conquered death in his resurrection. Now death is the door through which believers enter into eternal life. God proclaims the *"blessedness"* of all who walk through that door. Our grieving hearts cause us to view death as a permanent loss. God tells us the death of a believer looks different to him. God sees the death of a believer as a "blessed" event. The apostle Paul echoed that idea when he said, *"For me to live is Christ! To die is gain!"*

Read Revelation 14:1-20

VISION OF THE HARVEST OF THE EARTH

In the sixth vision of the Vision of Seven Visions, God fixes our eyes on the most important event in human history, the day on which all mankind will gather to give an account to the Lord who made us. The Vision of the Harvest of the Earth reveals the Judgment Day. John sees the Lord Jesus, the Lamb seated on a cloud. He wears the crown of gold as the *"King of kings and Lord of lords."* Strong and irresistible as our enemies might be, there is a greater power over them that sets limits and boundaries and outcomes. That power is the Lamb seated on a cloud, ruling the universe for the benefit of his church. From the perspective of the enemies, the most ominous detail in this vision is the *"sharp sickle"* the Lamb holds in his hand.

As John watches in wonder, an angel comes from the Temple and speaks in a loud voice. *Then another angel came out of the temple and called in a loud voice to him who was sitting on the cloud, "Take your sickle and reap, because the time to reap has come, for the harvest of the earth is ripe."* (Rev. 14:15,16 NIV) There is a day of accounting. It is already marked with indelible ink on the calendar of eternity. When it comes the Lord himself will balance the scales of justice with one sweep of his sickle. God created and carried out the entire plan of salvation over a period lasting thousands of years with this one moment in mind. As God worked every day between the first and the second coming of Jesus to reach all people with the message of light, he did so fully aware that there would come a day when this work would be finished. On this last day God will fulfill his promises to his people and welcome them into the heaven he has prepared for them. Notice that the Vision of the Harvest is revealed in two steps. The Lamb on the cloud begins the process by harvesting his grain. Then, with the people of God safely gathered to their eternal rest at the side of the Lamb, God reveals the second harvest of the grapes of wrath.

Make no mistake as to what awaits this earth. This will be for the unbeliever a terrible day of judgment and that day will never end. John sees another angel appear with a sharp sickle. This angel receives a command from the altar of God. *"Take your sharp sickle and gather the clusters of grapes from the earth's vine, because its grapes are ripe."* [19] *The angel swung his sickle on the earth, gathered its grapes and threw them into the great winepress of God's wrath.* (Rev. 14:17-19 NIV) What awaits the followers of the beasts and the Dragon is the *"winepress of God's wrath."* In one of the most horrifying pictures of God's wrath in the Bible, John describes the river of blood that will flow from this event, a river as deep as a *"horse's bridle"* and as long as *"1,600 stadia."* There will be no reprieve. There will be no second chance. This will be a moment when all hope is lost for the enemies of God.

This sixth vision brings the picture into complete focus for believers. The visions make it clear that there will always be three savage enemies in this world that intend harm to God's people and to all the people of this earth. These enemies will have great power and they will bring suffering into the lives of all who follow the Lamb. However, the visions also reveal that *"their time is short."* While these beasts roam the earth and spread their suffering, the Lamb will rule over them and limit what they achieve. God has already appointed a day in the calendar of earth events on which he will settle the score. Evil will not triumph. Justice will be done. And until that day the Lamb will watch over his people and make all things work for their good. This Lamb is our comfort as we walk through each day in this dangerous world.

Read Revelation 15:1-8

THE SEVENTH VISION

With that truth as our daily compass, we are ready to see the *"final vision"* of the Seven Visions which God records in Revelation chapter fifteen. Here God employs a literary technique called "foreshadowing." Writers and movies and television stories use this technique to alert readers and viewers to the fact that something is about to change. God does this with the story that is the Revelation. With chapter fifteen God brings to a conclusion the Vision of the Seven Visions and he opens the door to the next truth he wants us to see.

The seven visions within this segment connect to each other by the opening phrase *"and I saw."* This is how we know that the vision in chapter fifteen forms the conclusion to the Vision of Seven Visions. John begins the description with these words. *I saw in heaven another great and marvelous sign: seven angels with the seven last plagues—last, because with them God's wrath is completed.* (Rev. 15:1 NIV) In the Vision of the Seven Seals God used the seventh seal to introduce the Seven Trumpets of Judgment. God follows that same pattern here, using the seventh vision to introduce the next vision, the Vision of the Seven Bowls of Wrath.

God is "foreshadowing" the final truths he is going to reveal. In the first fourteen chapters of the Revelation we learned the truths that explain what we see every day in this world and our purpose in each day. We know what will happen until Jesus returns. We know why these things will happen as the spiritual war plays out on the visible landscape of our lives. Beginning with Revelation chapter fifteen, God leads us to the next step. The Lord uses this final vision of the Seven Visions to turn our eyes in the direction of the end he has planned.

The Vision of the Seven Bowls of Wrath will direct our attention specifically to the end God has planned for those who oppose him. God will fill the lives of unbelievers with hardship and suffering, and each new hardship will carry the message of God's judgment and wrath. Notice God calls these the *"last plagues"* because they will complete the wrath of God. We are not dealing with a world that is running in a circle without final solution. We walk a linear path through this world advancing toward a day of reckoning set by God himself. The seven angels carry the news of the final conclusion.

John sees the location from which the final solution will come, namely heaven itself. In this vision he sees the celebration that takes place as God reveals his plan to pour his wrath on unbelievers in this world. John sees *"a sea of glass"* and standing beside that sea are the saints of God safe at God's side in heaven. In their hands these saints hold *"golden harps."* Playing these harps they raise their voices in song. John describes their song as the *"song of Moses"* reminding us of the victory song the Israelites sang when God delivered them from the Red Sea. Then John calls it the *"song of the Lamb"* referring to the victory song God's people would sing in celebration of God's deliverance on Easter Sunday. By combining these two songs in this way, John is hearing a song the people of the Old Testament and the people of the New Testament sang to give glory to God who delivers his people from their enemies. With this song they are celebrating the *"great and marvelous sign"* that John saw and what it portends.

The heavens rejoice in the name and glory of the Lord for three reasons. First, God is holy and deserving of the praise of all, a praise that the sinful world gives instead to the beasts of evil. Second, God's works are great and marvelous. If the world is impressed with the power of the Beast of the Sea, it will be much more impressed by the power of the Lord. Third, the works of the Lord are *"righteous and true."* While the Dragon and his helpers fill the world with actions of evil, the acts of God are good and demonstrate his goodness. Primarily here, God demonstrates that goodness by opposing evil and bringing it to justice.

John reveals the thing that causes them to celebrate. *After this I looked and in heaven the temple, that is, the tabernacle of the Testimony, was opened. ⁶ Out of the temple came the seven angels with the seven plagues. They were dressed in clean, shining linen and wore golden sashes around their chests.* (Rev. 15:5-6 NIV) John sees seven angels descending from the throne of God. These seven angels carry the justice of God into this world. The presence of the Dragon and the beasts on earth is an offense to God. Now from the very throne of God will come justice, the righting of the visible wrong under which the earth suffered for so long. Those in heaven celebrate as God's justice unfolds.

John calls our attention to the bowls the angels carried and to their contents. *Then one of the four living creatures gave to the seven angels seven golden bowls filled with the wrath of God, who lives forever and ever.* (Rev. 15:7 NIV) The golden bowls come from God himself. They contain the full anger and fury of the Lord toward the enemies that have blasphemed his name. Each angel receives a bowl of wrath and the charge to pour out this wrath on the unbelievers who walk on this earth.

John concludes the vision by describing the final scene in heaven. *And the temple was filled with smoke from the glory of God and from his power, and no one could enter the temple until the seven plagues of the seven angels were completed.* (Rev. 15:8 NIV) When God gave his Ten Commandments on Mt. Sinai, the mountain was covered with the smoke of God's glory. When Moses set up the Tabernacle in the desert, God filled the Tabernacle with his smoke as he entered it. When God appeared in his glory to call the prophet Isaiah to his ministry, Isaiah saw smoke fill the Temple of heaven, just as John does here. Now in heaven the glory of God fills the Temple and none can enter until the work of the Lord is finished and his enemies are defeated.

No matter how much evil you see in this world, never let yourself believe that people will get away with it. There is an end coming for those who live in rebellion. The enemies of God will be defeated once and for all. God will assure us of this truth every day as the angels pour out their bowls of wrath on the unbelievers.

Chapter Summary

The Vision of the 144,000 and the Lamb *assures us that as powerful as the savage enemies may be, God will keep his people safe and eventually bring them all to heaven. Not a soul will be lost.*

The Vision of the Three Angels *promises that God will make sure his Gospel message of hope is heard, even as the spiritual war rages. God will carry out his work of sharing his message of light with all people before it is too late. The angel flying in mid-air is a picture of this truth. At the same time the following two angels in the vision assure us that the enemies of God will be defeated, powerful as they might seem.*

The Vision of the Great Harvest *urges us to keep our eyes fixed on how this spiritual war will end. In the great harvest God will gather his own into the joys of heaven and he will consign those who opposed him to the winepress of his wrath.*

The three visions of Revelation in chapter fourteen balance the picture drawn by the three pictures in Revelation chapters twelve and thirteen. Combining the messages of these visions we have a balanced picture of the present and the future God has prepared for us. We will face three savage and powerful enemies until Jesus returns. But we need not fear. The Lord has marked his own and he will keep us safe. The enemies of God will ultimately be defeated. Finally, in the great harvest, God's justice will be accomplished.

CHAPTER TWELVE
The Vision of the Seven Bowls of Wrath

Revelation Chapter 16

Introduction

God's judgments in this world are linear, not circular. These events will not continue forever. There is a day of reckoning already marked on the eternal calendar. Toward that day and its results the Lord now turns our attention, beginning with the Vision of the Seven Bowls of Wrath in Revelation sixteen. The Vision of the Seven Bowls of Wrath revisits the subject God first introduced in the Vision of the Seven Trumpets. In both visions God makes it clear that he will use hardship, disaster and disease as mini-judgments to send a message to unbelievers and those who oppose him on this earth. The message is one of God's wrath toward the unbeliever and a warning to repent before it is too late.

God picks up this thread once again in his thought progression because it is God's plan now to show us how this judgment and wrath will end. With each new day we are one step closer to the great moment when all of creation will stand before the Lord and give an account. The Vision of the Seven Bowls of Wrath conveys a message of urgency by showing the results of the judgments as being more intense than in the Seven Trumpets of Judgment. All the creatures of the sea die when the bowl of wrath is poured out, whereas only one third died when the trumpet blew. God also adds the idea of inevitability in the Bowls of Wrath. The unbelievers face the clear wrath of God, yet in their agony they will not repent. Blasphemy is the only language they will speak to the very end. In this way God is foreshadowing the final result for all who oppose his name. God uses the Vision of the Seven Bowls of Wrath to introduce the discussion of the final outcome for all the enemies of the Lord.

Read Revelation 16:1-21

THE VISION OF THE SEVEN BOWLS OF WRATH

With the words of the three angels ringing in our ears promising the fall of Babylon and the coming of the great harvest, we now turn our attention to the impending judgment God has planned for those who dare to oppose him. In the Vision of the Seven Bowls of Wrath God reveals the truth that the Day of Judgment will, in some ways, be no surprise at all. Long before that day arrives, the Lord will fill this earth from one end to another with warnings to the unbelievers that the day is approaching. The bowls vision reveals the truth we must always remember. The judgments of God will happen repeatedly in this world in many different forms. But each new disaster warns that time is running out. God is telling the unbelieving world that they are one step closer to the final judgment and their time is short. This is the message God reveals in the vision recorded in Revelation sixteen.

Even a cursory reading of the Vision of the Seven Bowls of Wrath will find many similarities between this vision and the Vision of the Seven Trumpets of Judgment. Both visions address the same places on earth and the same people, the enemies of God. Both visions arise in the same way from the final element of the preceding vision. The Trumpets sounded from the opening of the seventh seal. The Bowls are poured from the unveiling of the seventh vision. God is sending essentially the same message with both visions.

This repeating pattern of warning is not unusual in the Bible. Joseph had two dreams that were strikingly similar when he was a boy, one depicting sheaves of grain bowing down and one depicting the sun and moon and stars bowing down. The Pharaoh in Egypt had two similar dreams, one with thin ears of grain eating fat ears and another with skinny cows eating fat cows. At that time Joseph told the Pharaoh that God had sent two similar dreams to note that the famine predicted would happen soon. King Nebuchadnezzar's dream of an image picturing four successive world empires was followed by Daniel's night vision of four beasts picturing the same historical event. In these examples God uses repetition to underscore the immediacy and urgency of his message.

Following that pattern, the Holy Spirit may well have listed these similar visions to deliver that same message of immediacy and urgency. This is made more likely by the introduction to the Revelation in which God says he is about to reveal *"what must soon take place."* However, the danger we face on this earth is complacency. It is true that the judgments of the Lord are all around us warning of the coming Judgment Day. Yet one day follows another. The days turn into weeks and then to months. The months turn into years. Before we blink our eyes, decades have passed and still the warnings of God continue and still the Judgment Day does not arrive. The Bowls of Wrath increase the intensity of the judgments pictured, sending the message to all that now is not the time for complacency. What God is revealing will happen *"soon"* and we had best live ready. This is the emphasis God adds to the picture with the Vision of the Seven Bowls of Wrath.

God used the seventh vision in the Vision of Seven Visions in chapter fifteen to introduce the seven angels in heaven. One of the four living creatures gave each of these angels a bowl filled with the wrath of God. Now, as chapter sixteen opens, we hear the voice of God coming from the altar with a clear command to these seven angels. *Then I heard a loud voice from the temple saying to the seven angels, "Go, pour out the seven bowls of God's wrath on the earth."* (Rev.16:1 NIV)

With that command, God begins to reveal his wrath toward unbelievers for all the world to see.

The first four angels pour out their bowls of wrath on the earth, the waters, and the heavens. With each new outpouring, the enemies of God are afflicted with disease and suffering and disaster. Two things stand out in the Vision of the Seven Bowls of Wrath, when comparing them with the Vision of the Seven Trumpets. Both visions picture the same events. However, the Bowls of Wrath add two things not contained in the Trumpets. The first is intensity. All the enemies of God are affected by the Bowls of Wrath, no one escapes. The second new thought is inevitability. The people face the wrath of God and they do not repent or turn from their evil ways. This intransigence signals their ultimate and certain demise. In spite of the clear and constant warnings of judgment from the Lord contained in the continuous outpouring of the Bowls of Wrath, the people will not repent. While the inhabitants of heaven rejoice in the justice of God as he begins to avenge the harm the people of darkness have caused the saints, the people with the mark of the beast do not respond to God's warning with repentance. Instead, John tells us this. *They were seared by the intense heat and they cursed the name of God, who had control over these plagues, but they refused to repent and glorify him.* (Rev. 16:9 NIV)

The fifth angel poured its bowl out on the throne of the beast. Remember how the people of the earth marveled at the power of the beast? Surely this beast held the answer to all the problems of life. Surely human government could solve all problems and overcome all obstacles, even God. To this very day we hear politicians building election campaigns on the promises of solutions they will bring to people's lives through government. But in the end we watch as the promises of this beast fail to ease the hardship of man and leave men in darkness and despair. In fact all too often the Beast of the Sea that is anti-Christian government adds to the darkness in this world. We will see governments support the most offensive actions, such as the killing of the unborn or the demonizing of one segment of society or another. In the face of this failure by the beast, we will see the people who bear the mark of this beast fail to turn to God in repentance. Instead they do the opposite. *Men gnawed their tongues in agony [11] and cursed the God of heaven because of their pains and their sores, but they refused to repent of what they had done.* (Rev. 16:10,11 NIV)

It is this hardened unbelief that sets the stage for the final days of this earth, days that God pictures in the actions of the sixth angel. When the angel pours the sixth bowl of wrath on the Euphrates River, the river to the east from which all the enemies of God in the Bible come, the river dries up. No longer will it block the way for the forces that mean harm to the people of God. John describes what happens next in these words. *Then I saw three evil spirits that looked like frogs; they came out of the mouth of the dragon, out of the mouth of the beast and out of the mouth of the false prophet. [14] They are spirits of demons performing miraculous signs, and they go out to the kings of the whole world, to gather them for the battle on the great day of God Almighty.* (Rev. 16:13,14 NIV)

God is describing the last days of this earth, the time he will later describe in Revelation chapter twenty as *"Satan's little season."* This is the time pictured in the Vision of the Two Witnesses when Satan killed the Two Witnesses and the world celebrated as they lay dead in the streets for three and one-half days. During these final days it will seem as if the whole world unites in its opposition to God and to those who dare to follow him. It will at that time appear as if those who love the darkness will overcome the people of God once and for all. John sees the evil spirits performing "great signs" to deceive the people with the mark of the beast, making them think they can oppose God and his people successfully. Jesus gave a similar warning about that moment in these words. *For false Christs and false prophets will appear and perform great signs and miracles to deceive even the elect—if that were possible.* (Matt. 24:24 NIV) If you wonder how such a thing could ever be, the Lord explains that here. The Dragon, the Beast of the Sea, and the Beast of the Earth will combine their lies into one powerful delusion so strong that all the enemies of God will turn against God with confidence, certain they can overcome him.

God goes so far as to name this approaching battle. *Then they gathered the kings together to the place that in Hebrew is called Armageddon.* (Rev. 16:16 NIV) This is the only time this word occurs in the Bible. Although John notes this is a Hebrew word, it is not found in the Old Testament. Some think the similar sounds in the word relate it to the mountainous area near the town of Megiddo in Israel. Several major battles, spiritual and physical, took place in this area in the history of Old Testament Israel. Some assume God uses an allusion to this area as a metaphor for the great battle that is to come near the end of time. However, with no historical reference clearly listed by God, our best approach may be to assign this unique word to the unique battle in the future which it represents, the moment when the final confrontation between God and the forces of evil take place.

This book of Revelation might appear to be filled with darkness for the forces of the Lord. But the Lord reveals the truth of what these days will bring and he urges us to live ready. What appears to be defeat for the Lord is actually a prelude to God's final victory. This great final battle is actually the harbinger of the promised coming of the Lord. *"Behold, I come like a thief! Blessed is he who stays awake and keeps his clothes with him, so that he may not go naked and be shamefully exposed."* (Rev. 16:15 NIV)

As proof of this, the seventh angel pours out his bowl and introduces a picture of the Judgment Day "from the perspective of the enemies of the Lord." *The seventh angel poured out his bowl into the air, and out of the temple came a loud voice from the throne, saying, "It is done!"* (Rev. 16:17 NIV) So says the Lord. The same God who pronounced the command that called the world into existence now calls the world to a final conclusion. God goes on in this vision to explain what is finished. *God remembered Babylon the Great and gave her the cup filled with the wine of the fury of his wrath.* (Rev. 16:19 NIV) No longer will the enemies oppose the Lord. No longer will they torment the saints of God. The judgment of the Lord will now become their final reality.

God describes the terror of that day in human terms. He speaks of an earthquake like the world has never seen or experienced before. John sees the fulfillment of the prophecy God made in the book of Hebrews. *"Once more I will shake not only the earth but also the heavens."* (Heb. 12:26 NIV) God speaks of hail from heaven in boulders that weigh 100 lbs each. He talks of islands and mountains that disappear from sight. But most of all, he describes the hard and anguished impenitent hearts of the people who bear the mark of the beast. For those who think that in the face of God's visible and impending wrath even the most hardened sinner would turn from his evil ways, John tells us it will not be so in the end. To the very end they curse the Lord and refuse to repent. Blasphemy is on the lips of those who bear the mark of the beast as the Lord sends them to an eternity of torment.

Chapter Summary

While the **Vision of the Seven Bowls of Wrath** *does not introduce much new information, it serves the purpose of focusing our attention on the final things Christians need to know if we are going to live successful lives in this world. God uses the final chapters of the Revelation to reveal how all things will come to an end. He will divide the discussion into two parts. First, in Revelation 16-20, God will show us how things will end for those who oppose his will. Then in Revelation 21 & 22 God will show us the end he has planned for those who are faithful to him. God uses Revelation chapter sixteen to introduce the topic of the destruction of God's enemies.*

CHAPTER THIRTEEN
The Vision of the Great Prostitute

Revelation Chapter 17

Introduction

God has revealed a lot about this world in our study of the Revelation. From the visions God has drawn we now know what will happen. God will use each day to reach all people with the light of Jesus Christ. During that time, all people -- even those who believe in Jesus -- perhaps especially those who believe in Jesus -- will face much hardship and tribulation as they walk through life. We also know why this will happen. There is an angry Red Dragon who means us harm. All that is left to learn is how all this will end. That is the final story God reveals in the last six chapters of the Revelation.

First of all, God tells the story of the sure and certain end for the enemies of his light. These visions God records in Revelation chapters 17-20. Through them God makes it clear that no matter how strong the enemies might seem, or how successful they appear to be, in the end God will vanquish all who tormented his people and attacked his church and fought against his message of light and hope.

Read Revelation 17:1-6

THE GREAT PROSTITUTE

In Revelation chapter seventeen we meet a new enemy, a woman whom God calls the Great Prostitute. All Christians in the New Testament, regardless of the time in which they live, need to understand this vision. The fact is, all Christians will see this woman. Yet identifying this woman has not been an easy thing to accomplish. Revelation chapter seventeen generates as much confusion among Bible students as any other chapter in the Revelation. If we are going to avoid this confusion and, at the same time, understand the message God is revealing we must employ the Bible reading skills we acquired as we began our study. We must pay attention to the words God speaks and to the details he reveals. Most important, we must keep constantly in mind that what we encounter in Revelation seventeen is a description of a picture. Therefore we must approach it as we would approach a painting.

Pictures are filled with thousands of small details of color and form. An artist combines these details on his canvas to tell a story or to present an idea with which we all can identify. If we are going to understand the message of the artist, we must make sure we examine the picture as a whole unit. If we allow ourselves to be distracted by one detail or another in the picture, we will in the end lose sight of what the artist is saying in his painting. Always look at the whole picture! This warning is critical to our understanding of the message of God in the pictures he drew in the Revelation.

As chapter seventeen opens, one of the angels who held one of the Seven Bowls of Wrath introduces John to a new vision. *Come, I will show you the punishment of the great prostitute, who sits on many waters.* (Rev. 17:1 NIV) The woman catches our eye immediately. God describes her as *"the great prostitute"* and in that description we find the key to the meaning behind this picture. Remember the faithful pregnant woman we met in Revelation chapter twelve? We learned at that time that the woman of chapter twelve was the faithful church of God, pregnant with the promise of the Savior. In contrast to her, this woman in chapter seventeen is the unfaithful church of God who offers a message the world wants to hear, and she does so for personal gain. In the eyes of the world, this woman sits within the church of God and appears to serve God. Yet in God's eyes she is a traitor, a Great Prostitute, who uses God's name in the world to work for her own gain and against God.

This vision carries a warning for us. As we wait for Jesus to return, God's people in every age will be plagued by the sight of this visible church gone astray. Instead of offering God's light and his message of salvation, this apostate church will offer a message to please the dark world as she seeks gain for herself. In the process, instead of making disciples for God from all nations as God commanded his church on earth, this woman will make disciples of darkness while acting outwardly in the name of God.

The presence of this woman will be wide-spread in this world. God reveals that in his vision as the angel points out that the Great Prostitute *"sits on many waters."* Later in the chapter God explains this picture. *The waters you saw, where the prostitute sits, are peoples, multitudes, nations and languages.* (Rev. 17:15 NIV) This woman loves the things of the world. She speaks the language of the world, offering darkness as if it is light. As a result, the people of the world support her and follow her. This woman will have followers in every land and in every nation until Jesus returns. Pretending to speak for God from within what appears to be the church of God, the influence of the Great Prostitute will extend to the highest reaches of power in this world. *With her the kings of the earth committed adultery and the inhabitants of the earth were intoxicated with the wine of her adulteries.* (Rev. 17:2 NIV) God pictures a world drunk on the wine of her lies.

This evil woman will be a great and constant threat to believers in this world. God demonstrates that in this vision by picturing the woman riding the scarlet beast. We met this beast in Revelation chapter thirteen and identified it as a "political beast" which is "anti-Christian government." The Great Prostitute rides this beast and works with him to enhance his power and to foster his acceptance by the people of the world. This she does even though the essence of the beast is to blaspheme God whom she says she serves.

God tells us that one of the clear identifying characteristics will be her vast wealth. This woman resides within the Christian church. She passes herself off as someone who stands for God while she leads people further into darkness. And she has huge and obvious wealth. The Great Prostitute wears the crimson colors of the beast. She adorns herself with precious stones and drinks from golden goblets. The cup she offers the world to drink is filled with adulterous lies enticing people to be unfaithful to God.

Her betrayal of the Lord is a great offense to the Lord and in his eyes earns her a lasting title until Jesus returns. *Babylon the Great, the Mother of Prostitutes!* (Rev. 17:5 NIV) In the Old Testament Israel's greatest enemies came from the east, from the direction of the city of Babylon. Over time the city of Babylon became known to God's people as the seat of evil. Now God reveals that this woman has become the New Testament Babylon. She is the enemy of God's people, and her betrayal of the Lord brings much suffering to the lives of God's people. John sees this woman *...drunk with the blood of the saints.* (Rev. 17:6 NIV) It is critical that Christians learn to recognize this woman and the danger she brings. Every Christian will see this woman and the beast that she rides, and every Christian will need to learn to guard against her.

Read Revelation 17:7-14

The Mystery of the Beast and the Prostitute

Remember that God draws the visions or pictures of the Revelation to tell us things he wants us to learn, just as any artist would. God helps us focus on the things that matter as we look at each picture so we will be able to recognize which elements of each picture carry his message. In this case, God tells us he created this picture to reveal two "mysteries" to us. Now he will explain the mystery of the woman and the mystery of the beast. The first mystery the angel addresses is that of the Beast of the Sea.

We already know that this beast is the political beast we met in Revelation chapter thirteen. There we learned that the Beast of the Sea represents anti-Christian government. God revisits this image to make sure we understand this simple truth. The "past" which Christians have experienced, filled with persecution by anti-Christian government, will also be the "future" Christians will experience until the Lord returns. What has been will be! God conveys this idea in a most unusual way. God tells us that the Beast *"once was, now is not, and will come up out of the Abyss."*

The power of the beast seems to wax and wane. Sometimes it will appear strong and overpowering as it persecutes the people of God. Sometimes it will appear that it has lost all such power, almost as if *"it was not."* But it will always come back to life again as history moves from one chapter to the next. This constant return to power after it appeared it was defeated will greatly impress the unbelievers in this world. *The inhabitants of the earth whose names have not been written in the book of life from the creation of the world will be astonished when they see the beast, because he once was, now is not, and yet will come.* (Rev. 17:8 NIV) The people with the mark of the beast will be continually amazed at the resilience of the beast, convinced that nothing, not even God, can stand against it.

In this vision God wants to make sure his people understand that this anti-Christian power of government which has been in their lives to this very moment *(remember John receives this vision while in exile on the Island of Patmos),* will continue in the future until Jesus returns. God makes that point within the picture using the *"seven heads"* of the beast as a metaphor. God tells us *"the seven heads … are seven kings."* Of these seven, God tells us *"five have fallen,"* meaning five of these kings have already come and gone in earth history. That is the past. Of these seven, *"one is"* at the moment. One of these kings reigns right now in John's day. That is the present. God says there is one *"who has not yet come"* and when he does come he must remain for *"a little while."* That is the future.

Students of the Revelation encounter problems in trying to understand this picture when they assume God is speaking of seven specific kings. Making this mistake, some Bible students try to identify seven emperors from the Roman Empire as being the kings God is describing. In the end all who try this approach fail. There is no way to make the Roman emperors align with what God is describing. The seven kings mentioned here cannot refer to seven specific Roman emperors. A better understanding of what God is revealing here is found in the Old Testament. The *"seven kings"* to which the vision refers represent seven "kingdoms or empires," five of which appeared in the Old Testament.

God is describing the past with the different heads on this beast. God recounts the world empires from the time of the Old Testament and the harm they brought on his people. Egypt was the first empire that had fallen, an empire which enslaved God's people for 400 years. The Assyrians came next, carrying the ten northern tribes of Israel into captivity. Then came the Babylonians who carried Judah into exile for seventy years. When the Persians overthrew the Babylonians, they dominated the people of God even as they allowed them to return to the Promised Land. Then came the Greeks who brought oppressive rule to the Jewish people, desecrating their worship at times. Each of these empires in one way or another brought harm to the people of God. That was the past. The Roman Empire is the *"one who is"* at the time of John. The final head represents one who is *"yet to come."* That is the future.

Behind all these empires that come and go is the Beast of the Sea himself. The angel speaking to John describes him as an eighth king. God describes him as one who *"once was and now is not."* His presence and power on this earth waxes and wanes with the deaths and the reappearances of each new kingdom. The point that God is making is that the past experienced by the Lord's lampstands in this world has been dominated by the beast that works through governments to persecute them. This has been their common experience. In every form of government, in every world power, Christians have experienced hardship at their hands. It is all the beast and always the beast. That is the past. Now God goes on to tell us that this will also be the future until Jesus returns. God tells us that the *"ten horns"* on the beast represent *"ten kings who have not yet received a kingdom."* These kings are yet to come in the future, and when they do, God tells us each will rule for *"one hour."*

Note the number "ten." In the Revelation God uses the number ten to represent *"completeness."* When God describes ten kings who will rule for ten hours, he is describing the complete future Christians will face in this world. God is telling us that the future will be filled with anti-Christian governments just as the past has been. And just as it was in the past, so in the future it will be the beast who directs these governments to use their power to oppose the plan of God for this world.

This is the final point God makes. These kingdoms *"receive authority"* from the beast. This authority has only one purpose. As they did in the past, so the kingdoms will *"wage war against the Lamb"* in the future. Their goal will be to harm the people of God and to oppose his kingdom. These enemies combine to war against the Lamb and against his followers. In the end, the Lamb will overcome them.

Read Revelation 17:15-18

THE DEMISE OF THE GREAT PROSTITUTE

As the vision comes to an end beginning with verse 15, God returns to the main theme of this vision, the final end he has prepared for the enemies of his light. God tells us that the first enemy to meet her end will be the Great Prostitute. *The beast and the ten horns you saw will hate the prostitute. They will bring her to ruin and leave her naked; they will eat her flesh and burn her with fire.* (Rev. 17: 16 NIV) God reveals that the instrument of her demise will be the Beast of the Sea, the beast with whom she worked so closely. Driven by hatred, the beast will destroy this woman suddenly and completely. God goes on to reveal that this was his plan all along and he is the one who used the beast to accomplish this. *For God has put it into their hearts to accomplish his purpose by agreeing to give the beast their power to rule, until God's words are fulfilled.* (Rev. 17:17 NIV)

We dare not leave our study of this vision without identifying the Great Prostitute. The angel promised that he would reveal the mystery of the woman. To learn the identity of this woman we simply need to look at all the things God has revealed about her. In this vision God revealed six details about this woman.

First, God begins by calling this woman *"the Great Prostitute."* She stands in contrast to the faithful woman we met in Revelation chapter twelve. If that woman was the true church of God, then this Prostitute by contrast represents the unfaithful church of God. What makes her special is this Great Prostitute stands within the visible Christian church of God and passes herself off to the world as if she is of God. The world does not see her as a competing religion. The world sees her as part of the Christian religion. In truth, she is a Prostitute and not faithful to God.

Second, God told us this woman has wide influence throughout the world in every age until Jesus comes again. She *"sits on many waters"* and the waters are *"peoples and languages and nations."* This woman is a world-wide church with followers in every nation. From these two details, we are looking for a false Christian church that exists in every age until Jesus comes again and has followers all over the world.

Third, her influence extends to secular governments in that she works closely with them and rides on their back. Look for a seemingly Christian church with such world power that she relates to, negotiates with, and influences governments throughout the world in every age until Jesus returns. There are not many so-called Christian churches that fit that picture.

Fourth, she is very wealthy in the world's eyes. She drinks from gold cups, wears many precious stones, and is dressed in rich robes of crimson and purple.

Fifth, she is an enemy of God's truth and his people and works with the government rulers to persecute and even to kill the saints.

Sixth, she resides in a city built on seven hills, a city God symbolically names Babylon because she is the seat of evil. In John's day the *"city on seven hills"* was a common name for the capital of the Roman Empire, the city of Rome. In his first letter, Peter writes from Rome and calls her Babylon.

These are the six identifying marks revealed in the vision. In the fifteenth century at the beginning of the Reformation, Martin Luther read these marks and concluded that the Great Prostitute described here was the Roman Catholic Church. (see *"On the Babylonian Captivity of the Church"*, October 1520, Martin Luther) Our task as we live in this modern age is to consider Luther's conclusions to see if they still are valid. As we compare the six marks of the Great Prostitute to the modern day Roman Catholic Church, the conclusions we reach are sobering. The Roman Catholic Church still has its head-quarters in Rome, just as it has always had throughout the ages. No so-called Christian church on earth is as intimately connected with secular governments as is the Church of Rome today. The Roman Catholic Church is the only church with actual ambassadors to nations. The Roman church is famous for its extensive earthly wealth, a wealth beyond calculation. Its leaders dress in the colors of crimson and purple and claim full authority alone to speak for God. Yet these same leaders oppose the Bible's teaching of salvation through faith in Jesus alone and condemn any who defend the light of God's truth. History is filled with stories recording the death of God's people for daring to oppose this powerful force.

Considering these details, we have to agree that this Great Prostitute forms a picture which matches the historical elements of the Roman Church. We see no reason to disagree with the understanding the Lutheran reformers reached five hundred years ago as they studied this vision. Therefore as we close the pages on this chapter, we wait with baited breath for the moment when God will fulfill the future he has predicted and the beast will turn on this woman to destroy her.

This chapter represents an important advance in the thought progression God follows in the Revelation. He has now opened the discussion to a new thought, namely the demise of the enemies once and for all. God is revealing the end he has prepared for all who will oppose him. Revelation seventeen begins the discussion by detailing the end of this woman called the Great Prostitute.

CHAPTER FOURTEEN
Heaven and Earth React to the Death of the Prostitute

Revelation Chapter 18

Introduction

In our last segment we learned from the Vision of the Great Prostitute that this evil woman would be the first enemy to face the end God prepared for her. The next three chapters of the Revelation will complete the story of what will happen to all who oppose the Lord. In this world it looks as if the forces of the angry Red Dragon have a clear and growing advantage with each new day. We see violence growing and spreading among the people and nations throughout the world. The visions we are about to see will remind us of what our eyes cannot see. God remains in full control in this world. His plan guides what happens. According to that plan, those who walk in the darkness of the Red Dragon are moving closer to a date with eternal punishment.

Read Revelation 18:1-24

THE WORLD MOURNS THE DEATH OF THE PROSTITUTE

After reading so much of the Revelation, it is clear that God has founded many of the visions of the Revelation on the visions of the ancient prophets of the Old Testament. His purpose in doing this is to help us see the continuity of the plan he made in the Garden of

Eden. God is not revealing a new plan in the Revelation visions. He is completing a plan started long ago. The Old Testament connection with many of the visions of the Revelation reminds us of this long term activity of God on the pages of human history. So it is no surprise that in the vision John records in Revelation eighteen, we can hear the echoes of the ancient prophets Isaiah and Jeremiah predicting the fall of ancient Babylon.

In the Old Testament Babylon became the symbol of all the enemies of God's people, the very seat of evil. It was Isaiah who first predicted ultimate doom for this evil city. *Babylon has fallen, has fallen!* (Isaiah 21:9 NIV) Isaiah was the first to point out the arrogance of the evil rulers of Old Testament Babylon and the false security that pride created. *Now then, listen, you wanton creature, ... saying to yourself, '... I will never be a widow or suffer the loss of children.' ⁹ Both of these will overtake you in a moment, on a single day: loss of children and widowhood.* (Isaiah 47:8,9 NIV) It was Jeremiah who urged the people of God to flee ancient Babylon because of the coming destruction. *Come out of her, my people! Run for your lives! Run from the fierce anger of the LORD.* (Jer. 51:45 NIV) Jeremiah was the first to draw the picture of a deserted city to reveal the final overthrow of Babylon. *So desert creatures and hyenas will live there, and there the owl will dwell. It (Babylon) will never again be inhabited or lived in from generation to generation.* (Jer. 50:39 NIV) In the vision God gave John in Revelation eighteen, God revisits the language of the ancient prophets to announce the fall of the Great Prostitute, symbolized by the metaphor of a New Testament "Babylon." Reading Revelation eighteen against the backdrop of the ancient prophecies deepens our understanding that God is revealing the completion of an ancient plan to crush his enemies.

As the new vision in Revelation chapter eighteen unfolds, John sees a mighty angel appear out of heaven announcing with a loud voice ... *"Fallen! Fallen is Babylon the Great!"* (Rev. 18:2 NIV) The angel is reacting to the truth God already revealed in Revelation chapter seventeen. The ultimate destruction of this evil woman, the Great Prostitute, is certain. Her end is not caused by the will of man or an accident of political power shifting. It is caused by the judgment of God. God will destroy her for the lies she told and the damage she did to the souls God treasures.

For all the nations have drunk the maddening wine of her adulteries. The kings of the earth committed adultery with her, and the merchants of the earth grew rich from her excessive luxuries. (Rev. 18:3 NIV) This Great Prostitute used the name of God to tell lies that sanctioned the evil behavior of those who lived in darkness. This evil woman provided a license to the kings and merchants of this earth to indulge in immorality, greed and selfishness as they pursued earthly wealth and power. She put God's stamp of approval on their sinful behavior. Protected by that moral permission, the people of the world reaped earthly rewards. The kings and the nations they led followed this woman down the path of unfaithfulness to the God who made them. This was her sin.

Now this evil woman stands in the shadow of God's imminent judgment. Therefore the angel warns the people of God that Babylon is no place for them. Those who walk with this Great Prostitute face the danger of *"sharing in her sins."* Those who walk too closely with this woman will also face the danger of *"receiving … her plagues."* This call of the Lord is a sobering warning to all of God's people. There will be those in the family of God who will think that showing kindness, acceptance or cooperation with the Great Prostitute might be a better way to open the door to winning her over to the light. In truth such a path is folly. The essence of this woman is evil. Those who stay in her presence will share the judgment God is about to pour out upon her.

The angel notes the excessive arrogance of this woman. The Great Prostitute walks before the world in the clothing of the *"bride of Christ"* even as she tells her lies. This clothing makes her think she stands in the favor of God. At the same time through the lies she tells in God's name, she pleases the nations of the world and their rulers. This Prostitute tells them that their greedy, selfish and immoral behavior is acceptable before God. Therefore she thinks the world favors her as well. As a result, this woman lives with a false sense of security, thinking nothing will harm her as she enjoys what she thinks is the favor of God and man. The angel announces that for this arrogance God has prepared a breathtaking end for this evil woman. *In her heart she boasts, 'I sit as queen; I am not a widow, and I will never mourn.' ⁸Therefore in one day her plagues will overtake her: death, mourning and famine. She will be consumed by fire, for mighty is the Lord God who judges her.* (Rev. 18:7,8 NIV) Her demise will come so suddenly and so quickly it will leave the people of the world in shock as they watch.

The angel records the world's disbelief. The kings of the world, the merchants of the world, and the sea captains of the world … all express the same reaction. All of them grieve over their loss, for in her presence they all enriched themselves. To them it seems impossible to comprehend that someone so rich and so strong could so suddenly be destroyed. In her demise those who consorted with this woman sense a spiritual warning of some kind. They are shocked at how rapidly and unexpectedly she has fallen. *Terrified at her torment, they will stand far off and cry: "Woe! Woe, O great city, O Babylon, city of power! In one hour your doom has come!"* (Rev. 18:10 NIV)

At issue here is the foundation the Great Prostitute built for the people of this world. The Prostitute granted the world a moral license to build their worldly success on a foundation of greed and selfishness, assuring them God was pleased with them in spite of their actions. Now God's judgment on this woman and her lies is unmistakable. If she incurred God's wrath in this way, surely that same wrath is coming for those who followed her lies. Thus the world grieves her loss and fears the future.

The inhabitants in heaven have the opposite reaction. For them the demise of this terrible woman is cause for celebration. *Rejoice over her, O heaven! Rejoice, saints and apostles and prophets! God has judged her for the way she treated you.* (Rev. 18:20 NIV) This evil woman suffers the punishment she deserves for the crimes she has committed against the Lord and his people, and heaven celebrates the victory of the Lord.

With a chilling sense of finality, the mighty angel performs an action that symbolizes the demise of this evil woman. He takes a huge boulder and throws it into the sea. *Then a mighty angel picked up a boulder the size of a large millstone and threw it into the sea, and said: "With such violence the great city of Babylon will be thrown down, never to be found again."* (Rev. 18:21 NIV) This is the final word from the Lord. This terrible woman will be fully destroyed never to rise again. God shows us the streets of Babylon deserted and empty. God records the sounds that will never be heard again. No music is played. No workmen are producing products. No light is shining anywhere. The sounds of lives being lived, weddings being celebrated, are missing.

God ends this vision with a final listing of the crimes of this Great Prostitute. God entrusted his church with the job of *"making disciples of all nations."* Instead the Great Prostitute led people further away from God, making them *"disciples of darkness."* She convinced the world that the darkness was light. She told them that this path was pleasing to God. She made their unfaithfulness seem as if it was faithfulness. For all these sins in this great spiritual war, she now will be punished.

When the martyred saints in the Vision of the Seven Seals cried out asking the Lord to avenge their loss, the Lord told them they must *"wait a little longer."* Now God adds to this message telling them and us that we will not have to wait forever. The enemies of God will not stand forever. The spiritual war is coming to an end. Slowly but surely the Lord Jesus is putting all his enemies under his feet. The woman called Babylon is the first sign of this ultimate end. God goes on in the next chapter to reveal the end he has planned for the two beasts that assisted the Dragon in his war against the Lord and his people.

CHAPTER FIFTEEN
The End for the Two Beasts

Revelation Chapter 19

Read Revelation 19:1-10

THE WEDDING SUPPER OF THE LAMB

In Revelation eighteen the angel invited the inhabitants of heaven to celebrate the demise of the Great Prostitute. In chapter nineteen John sees heaven respond. John hears a mighty roar from the heavens as all its inhabitants seem to shout together, *"Hallelujah!"* Then the same voices explain the reason for their celebration. *"Hallelujah! Salvation and glory and power belong to our God, ²for true and just are his judgments. He has condemned the great prostitute who corrupted the earth by her adulteries. He has avenged on her the blood of his servants."* (Rev. 19:1,2 NIV) This was the moment for which all creation has been waiting. The demise of the Great Prostitute is the sign all have been eagerly anticipating. The enemies of God will be defeated.

The 24 elders and the four living creatures take the lead in the worship. Before long John hears the heavenly throng enthusiastically announcing the *"wedding of the Lamb."* At the center of the celebration is the bride, dressed in what John describes as *"fine linen."* John is quick to explain that this gown was made of *"the righteous acts of the saints."* In Matthew 25 Jesus told a parable about the Last Day. He pictured the Father welcoming the saints into heaven while praising them for the way they helped God in times of need. When the saints questioned what God was describing, God told them that what they had done in faith for those in need, they had done for him. Faith sets Christians free to serve God. On the last day those acts of service to God will serve as evidence of the faith in the hearts of believers. Through faith in Christ, God treats those actions as if they had been perfect acts of love for him. Hence, God tells us here that the saints of God are clothed in *"righteous acts"* as they attend the victory celebration of the Lord.

As John stands with the angel watching this heavenly event, the angel speaks. *Then the angel said to me, "Write: 'Blessed are those who are invited to the wedding supper of the Lamb!'" And he added, "These are the true words of God."* (Rev. 19:9 NIV) No invitation in the course of a person's life is as important to secure as this invitation. Attending this great wedding supper is the goal of every human life. God wants all people to attend this feast. God created a plan of salvation so all could attend simply by trusting Jesus as their Savior. Those who walk by faith in the Son of God will be present at this feast. Their presence is the one true measure of a successful life.

John was overwhelmed by what he saw. He fell at the angel's feet in order to worship him. The angel responded in these words. *Do not do it! I am a fellow servant with you and with your brothers who hold to the testimony of Jesus. Worship God! For the testimony of Jesus is the spirit of prophecy.* (Rev. 19:10 NIV) The angel reminds John that he is just the messenger. Jesus, and only Jesus, merits our worship.

Read Revelation 19:11-21

The Lamb Defeats the next Three Enemies

With this message, a new vision unfolds. John sees the rider on the White Horse. His name is called ... *Faithful and True.* (Rev. 19:11 NIV) We have met this rider before. When the Lamb opened the first of the Seven Seals, we saw this White Horse and its rider begin its ride throughout the world. At that time the rider was not identified. Now God reveals the rider's identity to us. John tells us the rider had *"blazing eyes"* and *"many crowns."* He wore *"robes dipped in blood."* Those following him were *"dressed in fine linen, white and clean."* Out of his mouth came a *"sharp sword."* But most revealing of all was his name. John tells us his name was *"the Word of God."* This is the name John used in the Gospel of John to identify Jesus. From this we know that the rider on this White Horse is Jesus himself. He leads an army of the righteous, each dressed in robes he has provided for them. At the head of this army, Jesus rides forth to carry out the final defeat of his enemies. As this army rides forward into the final battle, the battle we know as Armageddon, John sees the most chilling vision of all.

John sees an angel in the sun. This angel issues a blood chilling invitation to the birds flying in the air. He invites them to the *"great supper of God"* and he announces the menu. *"Come, gather together for the great supper of God, ¹⁸ so that you may eat the flesh of kings, generals, and mighty men, of horses and their riders, and the flesh of all people, free and slave, small and great."* (Rev. 19:17,18 NIV) This is an invitation to a feast, but not a feast like the one we just saw. The angel invites the birds of the air to come and eat the flesh of God's defeated enemies as they lay dead. The Lamb and his army have destroyed the enemy and now the angel invites the birds to come and devour the dead bodies.

No one will be able to withstand the power of the Lamb. Even the terrible beasts who assisted the Dragon must answer for what they have done. John announces the news. *But the beast was captured, and with him the false prophet who had performed the miraculous signs on his behalf.* (Rev. 19:20 NIV) In the end Jesus will take these terrible creatures captive and he will punish them as they deserve, along with all who followed them. The Beast of the Sea and the False Prophet are thrown into the Lake of Fire.

The vision ends with that terrible sight, birds eating the flesh of the people who bore the mark of the beast. With the fall of the Prostitute and the deaths of the two beasts and those who followed them, there is only one enemy that remains, namely the Dragon himself. God reveals his end with the visions John records in Revelation chapter twenty.

CHAPTER SIXTEEN
The End for the Dragon

Revelation Chapter 20

Introduction

The visions we are about to study in Revelation chapter twenty bring this segment of the Revelation to a conclusion. Beginning with the visions in chapter sixteen, God has been revealing how all things will come to an end. For the last three chapters, God has been revealing the judgment he planned for his enemies. So far we have learned the end God ordained for the Great Prostitute, the Beast of the Sea, the Beast of the Earth whom he called the False Prophet, and those who bear the mark of the beast. One last enemy remains. We know the final judgment for all those who aided the Dragon. In Revelation chapter twenty God reveals the end he has planned for the Dragon himself.

Read Revelation 20:1-3

THE BINDING OF SATAN

In this chapter we find one of the most well known visions of the book of Revelation. It begins with the appearance of an angel descending from heaven with a key to the Abyss in one hand and a great chain in the other. The Abyss is a metaphor for hell, the place of punishment God created for Satan and those who follow him. Both the chain and the key play a role in the message God wants us to learn from this vision. God's message in the picture lies in the next action of the angel.

John tells us the angel ... *seized the dragon, that ancient serpent, who is the devil, or Satan, and bound him for a thousand years.* (Rev. 20:2 NIV) We learned in Revelation chapter twelve that we live on the front lines of a spiritual war. The enemy forces that seek our harm in this war are led by a powerful angry Red Dragon. Now God tells us he has sent his angel to bind this enemy and to limit his power.

In this vision there are three metaphors that carry meaning: the Dragon, the chain, and the thousand years. The Dragon is a picture of Satan. We have seen this image before in the Revelation and it consistently carries this meaning. The chain which the angel carried contains the obvious message that God intends to "bind" Satan and to limit his power. On this everyone agrees. God defines the limitation in the vision with these words: *"to keep him from deceiving the nations anymore."* More than likely, the *"anymore"* in this case is a reference to conditions in the Old Testament as compared to the New Testament. In the Old Testament there was only one nation as a nation that believed in the true God. That nation, by God's grace, was Israel. But, in the New Testament as God spread his light throughout the world, whole nations became "Christian" in general.

The "chain" with which God "binds" Satan is an important metaphor in the vision. The "nature" of this "binding" creates an immediate question. God explains the limits imposed by the chain on the Dragon. He tells us it will *"keep him from deceiving the nations anymore."* Note that the "binding" coincides with the advent of the preaching of the Gospel message in the world. When Jesus completed the work of redemption with his death on Good Friday and his resurrection on Easter Sunday, the message of the Gospel was fully formed. Now all sin was forgiven. Now through faith in Jesus people had the power to resist the devil and his lies. This is the victory which we see the beings of heaven celebrate in Revelation chapter four and five as the Lamb enters heaven on Ascension Day. As long as the Gospel is preached in the world, that powerful message limits the power of Satan to deceive people. He still has great power and represents a great threat to all people, but that power is severely limited.

Recognizing that the metaphor of the "chain" pictures the preaching of the Gospel, also explains how Satan's power could increase just before the end of the world. Jesus predicted that as the world approaches the end of time there will be a great falling away from the Lord. *At that time many will turn away from the faith and will betray and hate each other, ¹¹ and many false prophets will appear and deceive many people. ¹² Because of the increase of wickedness, the love of most will grow cold, ¹³ but he who stands firm to the end will be saved.* (Matt. 24:10-13 NIV) With people falling away, the preaching of the Gospel will seem to disappear from the world and the devil's power to deceive will again grow. All of this leads us to conclude that the "chain" used to bind Satan was a picture of the Gospel message being preached throughout the world.

That brings us to the *"thousand years."* The *"binding"* of Satan marks the start of the *"thousand years."* Applying our 2nd principle of Bible reading, we find that other passages in the Bible help us fix this point to the time of Jesus' ministry on this earth. Remember when the Pharisees accused Jesus of using the power of Satan to cast out demons? Jesus used this picture to refute them. *Or again, how can anyone enter a strong man's house and carry off his possessions unless he first ties up the strong man? Then he can rob his house.* (Matt. 12:29 NIV) Jesus implies that he has bound the power of Satan and this fact accounts for Jesus' power over the demons. On another occasion when the disciples returned from a mission trip rejoicing in the work, Jesus made this statement. *He (Jesus) replied, "I saw Satan fall like lightning from heaven. ¹⁹ I have given you authority ... to overcome all the power of the enemy; nothing will harm you."* (Luke 10:18,19 NIV) From Jesus' words in the Bible, the limiting of Satan's powers was brought about by Jesus ministry on this earth. That is the start of the *"thousand years."*

Knowing when the *"thousand years"* began is just the first step. We need to have a clear grasp of the meaning God conveys with this picture if we are going to understand the full message of this vision. To do this we must remember that the *"thousand years"* is a picture, not a literal measurement of time. Here it is important to remember that God uses some numbers in the Revelation as metaphors. One of those "picture numbers" is the number ten. When God uses this number in the Revelation, he is presenting the picture of "completeness." The *"ten days of persecution"* in Revelation chapter two pictured a complete future of opposition facing the little church of Smyrna. The *"ten kings who have not yet received a kingdom"* and who would rule for *"ten hours"* in Revelation chapter seventeen pictures a complete future dominated by governments that will oppose God and his people, just as governments did in the past. Here God uses this number to tell us that for the majority of the New Testament time, Satan's power will be limited as God describes. Therefore, the *"thousand years"* is a picture of the time of the New Testament. It begins with the ministry of Jesus and it ends in the final days just before the Armageddon leading up to Judgment Day.

Two other points need to be addressed before we move on to the rest of chapter twenty. We should notice that while Satan's power is limited by the Gospel for the great majority of the New Testament, Satan remains a great threat to everyone in this world. Though the Gospel preaching limits Satan's power to deceive, Peter warns us that Satan is *"a roaring lion walking about seeking whom he may devour."* The Dragon and those who aid him will bring much suffering to God's church and to its people. However, they will not be able to destroy the church or keep it from performing its task of shining God's light into the darkness. The *"gates of hell"* will not prevail against the church of God.

The second thing we need to spend some time with is the false teaching centered around the concept of the millennium. Some Christians make the mistake of thinking that the *"thousand years"* is a literal measurement of time. They make this mistake by forgetting to look at this picture God has drawn with their "picture reading skills." The picture displays an angel coming down from heaven. The angel uses a chain to bind the serpent who is identified by God as the Devil. The serpent remains tied for *"a thousand years."* We know that the chain is not a chain. It is a metaphor. We know the snake is not a snake, it is a metaphor. Yet some Christians insist that the *"thousand years"* is a literal 1000 years. They pick this detail out of the picture and treat this detail as a measurable period of time that is 1000 years in length. These same people continue to treat the chain and the snake as metaphors. Only the *"thousand years"* is literal to them. Not only is this inconsistent approach to the vision an error in the way you read God's pictures. It also causes great confusion within the Christian church. From this confusion the various religious theories of the "millennium" find their origin. Christians who treat the *"thousand years"* as a literal measurement of time look forward to a future earthly kingdom of peace and joy which they say will last 1000 literal years.

Those who make this error fall into one of two general groups. One group believes Jesus will come again before Judgment Day and at that time he will establish an earthly kingdom of peace and joy in which he will reign with believers for 1000 years. This is called "pre-millennialism." Others think that under the steady influence of Christian teaching and practice, the world will gradually improve, eventually causing a period of peace and righteousness among people of this earth that will last 1000 years. Then, after that time, Christ will return for Judgment Day. This is called "post-millennialism." There are many variations built on these two general approaches. Some add in a "dispensational aspect," convinced God will convert all Jews to Christianity, and this mass conversion will usher in the millennium they anticipate.

All of these views are based on a literal reading of the *"thousand years"* in this vision, but all miss the point. This *"thousand years"* is a picture, a metaphor, not a literal measurement of time. God uses this picture to represent the great majority of time until Jesus returns again. It begins with Jesus' ministry and it ends with Satan being released in the days just before Judgment Day.

Read Revelation 20:4-6

THE SOULS WHO RULE WITH JESUS

Having told us that he will limit Satan's power during this time, God now goes on to reveal another truth about this same time period. *I saw thrones on which were seated those who had been given authority to judge.* (Rev. 20:4 NIV) John sees this happening during the thousand year period. *And I saw the souls of those who had been beheaded because of their testimony for Jesus and because of the word of God.* (Rev. 20:4b NIV) John sees people who have died, martyred for their faith. He is looking at the scene in heaven right now. There on the thrones John saw the Christians who have died. John says, *They came to life and reigned with Christ a thousand years.* (Rev. 20:4b NIV) It is important to pay careful attention to the words God uses. God clearly describes these people as the martyred saints in heaven. They had their lives taken from them for daring to stand with the Lord. Now John sees them in heaven, alive and reigning on thrones with Jesus himself.

As John's description of the vision continues, we need to make sure we understand three terms. The first is the *"rest of the dead."* John is talking about people who have died in unbelief. These unbelievers will not take part in the millennial reign with Christ. They will simply wait in the darkness of hell until the Judgment Day. John tells us the activity in heaven he is witnessing is called the *"first resurrection."* This term describes what the believers experience after they physically die. Believers awaken from physical death to find themselves in heaven, and there they rule with Christ until the day of the second coming. This first resurrection is a *"spiritual resurrection,"* one experienced by the soul while it remains separate from the body. The final term John uses that may sound strange to our ear is the *"second death."* This term is a reference to the final judgment which will send unbelievers to hell for eternity. Those who take part in the first resurrection are greatly blessed. The second death has no power over them.

This is the millennial kingdom which John sees in this vision. The *"thousand years"* begins with the ministry of Jesus on this earth. Jesus creates the good news of the Gospel. As that message is preached throughout the world, Satan's power to deceive is reduced. As the *"thousand years"* continue through the *"first resurrection"* when the believers in Christ come to the end of their physical life on this earth, they find thrones waiting for them in heaven. On these thrones believers rule with Jesus until the Judgment Day. So the world will continue until the time just before the end when the great falling away occurs and the Gospel preaching comes to an end. Then Satan will be free to deceive the world again. That terrible moment of Satan's success will serve as a warning that the end is near.

Read Revelation 20:7-10

THE DRAGON IS DESTROYED

The vision now directs our attention to those final days after the millennial kingdom of the Lord comes to its end. In these days Satan will meet his end. *When the thousand years are over, Satan will be released from his prison* [8] *and will go out to deceive the nations in the four corners of the earth—Gog and Magog—to gather them for battle.* (Rev. 20:7,8 NIV) Here we find another picture rooted in the ancient visions of the Old Testament. The prophet Ezekiel used these terms, *"Gog and Magog,"* to represent evil forces opposed to God. Gog was the leader of the evil force and Magog was the land in the north from which the enemies came. Ezekiel prophesied that God would destroy these enemies with fire and birds would feast on their bodies. This is the imagery God employs once again as he reveals the end he has ordained for Satan.

God has shown us the scene of this final battle called Armageddon a number of times in the Revelation. We first saw this battle when the angel blew the sixth trumpet of judgment. We saw this battle again in the Vision of the Two Witnesses when the Dragon killed the Two Witnesses and the world celebrated as their bodies were left to lay in the street for 3 ½ days. God was picturing these last terrible days in the sixth bowl of wrath when he showed us the three frog spirits gathering the enemies of the world for one final battle.

Now God gives us yet another look at this last terrible battle, the battle God already named Armageddon. God tells us it will occur *"when the thousand years are over"* at the end of time, just before Jesus returns. The Dragon and his helpers will deceive those who bear the mark of the beast into thinking they can once and for all defeat any who dare to stand for the Lord. God pictures them forming a huge army. *They marched across the breadth of the earth and surrounded the camp of God's people, the city he loves.* (Rev. 20:9 NIV) Their huge numbers and clear intent seem to spell doom for the people of God once and for all. These last days Jesus described in this way. *Those will be days of distress unequaled from the beginning, when God created the world, until now—and never to be equaled again.* (Mark 13:19 NIV) The final days will be horrible for the people of God. But, when all seems lost, *"... fire came down from heaven and devoured them."* When the enemies of God gather for battle to celebrate what they see as a certain victory, the Lord will destroy them once and for all.

At the same time, God will destroy the Dragon. This evil creature caused God's people great pain and suffering for thousands of years. He persecuted those who followed Jesus and even killed them. His end will be the same as that of the Beast of the Sea and the False Prophet. *And the devil, who deceived them, was thrown into the lake of burning sulfur, where the beast and the false prophet had been thrown. They will be tormented day and night forever and ever.* (Rev. 20:10 NIV) Never again will this enemy torment the people of God.

Never again will he accuse God's people or fill their lives with his lies. Now this enemy will face the punishment he deserves for eternity for the evil he has done. Thus will the last great enemy of the Lord and creation meet his end.

Read Revelation 20:11-15

THE FINAL JUDGMENT

When God throws the devil into the lake of fire for eternity, all the enemies will be defeated. Once that happens there is only one thing left to tend, the day of accounting. The vision John saw in chapter twenty ends as God reveals what will happen on that day. John sees a great white throne and on that throne sits the Lord God. This is a vision of the Judgment Day, the day on which every human being will be called to account for the life God gave that person.

Once the throne appears, John watches as all the dead are raised to life. This is clearly a physical bodily resurrection. The Bible very plainly teaches that all people will rise physically from the grave on this last day. *Do not be amazed at this, for a time is coming when all who are in their graves will hear his voice* [29] *and come out—those who have done good will rise to live, and those who have done evil will rise to be condemned.* (John 5:28,29 NIV) For those who would still question this idea, Job addresses the point graphically. *I know that my Redeemer lives, and that in the end he will stand upon the earth.* [26] *And after my skin has been destroyed, yet in my flesh I will see God;* [27] *I myself will see him with my own eyes—I, and not another.* (Job 19:25-27 NIV) All people will rise from the dead and each person will stand before the throne of God to give an account for the life God gave him. The determinative principle by which all will be judged will be the relationship they had with Jesus Christ. The vision revealed that God will produce evidence for all testimony on that day. The books John saw contain the record of every life lived. Each life will be examined for evidence of the presence of faith in Jesus

Christ. Proof of that faith will be seen in the actions of their lives and each person is judged according to what he has done. The evidence of their actions will confirm the faith in their hearts. For the believers that will be a day filled with joy. The entire world will hear their names read from God's Book of Life.

However, those whose names are not recorded in the Book of Life will find the day to be the beginning of an eternity of regret. *If anyone's name was not found written in the book of life, he was thrown into the lake of fire.* (Rev. 20:15 NIV) Those who wore the mark of the beast lived their lives separate from the Lord, ignoring his repeated calls to them to change their ways. Before the throne of the Lord they will see what they have lost. They will spend an eternity enduring the agony of being separated from God.

It is interesting that the last identified enemy to be defeated in the vision is not Satan, as we might expect. Instead it is death as God predicted through the Apostle Paul. *The last enemy to be destroyed is death.* (1 Cor. 15:26 NIV) All people on this earth take part in the "first death," the physical death that is the mortal's reality ever since sin entered the world. With the defeat of all enemies, death's reign over mortal man will come to an end.

For the child of God no news could be more welcomed. Paul looked forward to that day with this joyful thought. *"Where, O death, is your victory? Where, O death, is your sting?"*[56] *The sting of death is sin, and the power of sin is the law.* [57] *But thanks be to God! He gives us the victory through our Lord Jesus Christ.* (1 Cor. 15:55-57 NIV) But the "second death," an eternity in hell, is reserved only for those who did not believe in Jesus. Woe to those whose names were not found in the book. Great and everlasting will be their torment. Judgment, sure and certain, will be the end of the story for all who opposed the Lord and his light, all who lived their lives in darkness. This approaching verdict adds incentive for the lampstands of the Lord to shine their light into the darkness and to reach as many as possible *"before the night comes when no one can work."*

Summary

The Last Things, Part One

God used the visions of the Revelation in chapters 1-15 to reveal what would happen in this world and why it would happen. In Revelation 16-20 God has revealed what will happen to those who oppose his will. God introduced us to the Great Prostitute and then showed us the end he has planned for her. Following that God revealed the end for the Beast of the Sea, the False Prophet, and those who bear the mark of the beast. Finally in chapter twenty God showed us the end he has planned for Satan himself, the great Dragon.

CHAPTER SEVENTEEN
Three Visions of Heaven

Revelation Chapters 21 & 22

Introduction

Most of the pictures of heaven we draw in our minds are based on our earthly experiences. We like to think that if an activity on this earth gives us pleasure, like playing softball or golf or bowling or fishing or tending the garden, we hope that experience will be a regular feature in heaven. We tend to use our happiest times on earth as a kind of prism through which we try to picture the experience and the joy of heaven.

But the fact is, trying to view heaven in this earthly way will always leave us short of our goal. God warned us about this danger. *"No eye has seen, no ear has heard, no mind has conceived what God has prepared for those who love him"*— *[10] but God has revealed it to us by his Spirit.* (1 Cor. 2:9,10 NIV) The apostle Paul actually saw heaven. Yet as he tries to put into words what he saw, he gives up on the effort saying this. *I know a man in Christ who ... heard inexpressible things, things that man is not permitted to tell.* (2 Cor. 12:4 NIV) Heaven is so amazing it is impossible to describe to people whose experience is rooted in an earthly dimension. That is why the final visions of the Revelation in chapters twenty-one and twenty-two capture our immediate interest. In these last visions God speaks to the questions in our hearts. He draws pictures of heaven and through these pictures God reveals what we need to know about the future he has prepared for us.

Once again as we look at the visions John records we must remember that these visions are pictures which God drew. God is showing us heaven "as it looks to him." God draws three different pictures, two in Revelation twenty-one and one more in Revelation twenty-two. In Revelation twenty-one God pictures heaven as a beautiful bride dressed for her wedding day. This bride is the church as she looks to God. Then God draws a picture of the New Jerusalem, a city covered with gold and jewels and possessing immense wealth, again presenting our existence as it looks to God in heaven. The fact that God is drawing pictures is the critical element we must recognize if we are going to learn what God is teaching us. Keep that thought in your mind as you watch these visions unfold to see if you can understand the comfort God wants you to see. At the same time, as you watch the visions, see if you can identify the one clear difference between our existence on earth and our existence in the New Jerusalem. Each picture drawn by God highlights this "difference." Study the three pictures to see if you can identify the feature that explains the essence of heaven.

Read Revelation 21:1-27

THE NEW JERUSALEM

With the final two chapters of the Revelation, God turns our attention to the final truth we need to know to live in this world successfully. God has revealed the end he has planned for his enemies in Revelation 17-20. Now God is set to reveal the end he has planned for us and all who believe in Jesus. In chapter twenty-one God begins the discussion by showing us what our end will be and what our new home will be like. God calls it the *"New Jerusalem."*

John sees *"a new heaven and a new earth."* He explains that at the end of time *"the first heaven and the first earth had passed away."* Human beings were not the only ones cursed by sin in this world. The Bible reveals that the universe bears the curse as well. As such, the sin-cursed world is not a suitable place to form the home for the righteous in eternity. So on the last day God will destroy this universe. The Apostle Peter pointed to that event. *That day will bring about the destruction of the heavens by fire, and the elements will melt in the heat. ¹³ But in keeping with his promise we are looking forward to a new heaven and a new earth, the home of righteousness.* (2 Peter 3:12,13 NIV)

John notes one difference in the *"new earth"* God will create. He says that it did not have any *"sea."* God does not explain this change anywhere in the Bible. So, absent a clear explanation from the Lord, we will leave the explanation of this detail to the last day when the Lord himself will explain it to us.

Based on these seemingly clear statements from the Lord, many Bible students believe that God will destroy the heavens and the earth and then will create a new earth and heaven in which believers will live with the Lord forever. We should note, however, that there are Christians who see this a little differently. These Christians believe that God will remove his children from this physical universe and take them to be with him in heaven for eternity. These Bible students point to passages like the following. *For the Lord himself will come down from heaven, with a loud command, with the voice of the archangel and with the trumpet call of God, and the dead in Christ will rise first. ¹⁷ After that, we who are still alive and are left will be caught up together with them in the clouds to meet the Lord in the air. And so we will be with the Lord forever.* (1 Thess. 4:16,17 NIV) Relying on passages like this, many Christians look forward to an eternity in heaven which they view as the home of God. The Bible does not resolve the seeming conflict between the two visions. However, the vision John saw is filled with details which fill Christians on both sides of this discussion with joy and hope. We find this hope by looking more closely at the details God reveals with this picture of heaven.

I saw the Holy City, the new Jerusalem, coming down out of heaven

from God, prepared as a bride beautifully dressed for her husband.
³ And I heard a loud voice from the throne saying, "Now the dwelling of God is with men, and he will live with them. They will be his people, and God himself will be with them and be their God. ⁴ He will wipe every tear from their eyes. There will be no more death or mourning or crying or pain, for the old order of things has passed away." (Rev. 21:2-4 NIV) Whatever the circumstances, the essence of the future God has planned for us is built around his presence. God makes it plain that from the final day on, we will live with the Lord and he with us. Make sure you take note of this point. It is key to understanding what heaven is like.

God created each of us for a purpose. He designed us to serve him. Our happiness and contentment flow from our fulfillment of that purpose. On earth sin separates us from God and this separation is the root of our discontent. Our separation from God and from our intended purpose because of sin, explains why nothing on this earth is able to make us permanently happy. No matter how much pleasure a given earthly item or activity might give us, we know that the joy we gain will soon end as all pleasure does on this earth. This separation from God also explains why we participate in hobbies and sports and other forms of recreation. All these activities are diversions, meant to take our mind off of the emptiness that dwells in our hearts, the feeling that something is missing.

We were not created by God so that we could serve ourselves. We were created to be one with God, to serve him, and to fulfill his will. Even now in our sinful state, most likely the happiest moments we can identify in our lives are those moments where, for a brief period of time, we walked parallel with the will of God and served him instead of ourselves. The curse of sin has separated us from that purpose on this earth. In heaven there will be no separation. God tells us that in heaven he will dwell with us and we will dwell with him. No more separation from God! Instead we will be set free to live for God and to serve him. The result will be no more pain or sorrow or tears. For people created to live with God and to serve him, this new home will set us free to fulfill our eternal purpose. *And I—in righteousness I will see your face; when I awake, I will be satisfied with seeing your likeness.* (Psalm 17:15 NIV)

The second point God notes about our new home is that it is exclusive. There is a popular theological assumption today among some excessively optimistic people, that all who want to go to heaven, will go to heaven. Others go even further and believe that everyone will go to heaven. God makes it clear to John in this vision that only "thirsty" people go to heaven. Heaven depends on "what you drink."

Listen to how John puts it. *To him who is thirsty I will give to drink without cost from the spring of the water of life.* (Rev. 21:6 NIV) The water of life is the message of salvation through faith in Jesus. Only believers drink from this water. Unbelievers refuse. John sees that in the vision as well. *But the cowardly, the unbelieving, the vile, the murderers, the sexually immoral, those who practice magic arts, the idolaters and all liars—their place will be in the fiery lake of burning sulfur. This is the second death.* (Rev. 21:8 NIV) Those who do not drink the water of life will not be allowed to enter the New Jerusalem and to live with the Lord. All people will know who they are. Their actions will indicate clearly that the water of life was not part of their diet.

As the vision continues, God draws two pictures which reveal how pleased he will be with us in heaven and how we will look in his eyes. God introduces the idea first by picturing a beautiful bride on her wedding day. The angel calls her the *"bride, the wife of the lamb."* She represents the holy church of God, the woman we first met in Revelation twelve. God is showing us how we will look in his eyes on the day we enter heaven. For people who lived a lifetime aware each day that they were not what God wanted them to be, that they were offensive to the Lord and deserving of his wrath, this vision of the Bride is a wonderful relief. That is as the Lord intended. His message in the description of the beautiful bride is meant to convey the truth that through Christ, in God's eyes, we will be beautiful.

God blends this image of a bride into the next image of the Holy City to state this truth in a different way. The angel takes John to a high mountain and shows him the Holy City. John makes it clear that the city is a picture of God's holy church. It is marked with the number twelve, the number of the church. The twelve gates of the city bear the names of the twelve tribes of Israel. The twelve foundations on which the city is built bear the names of the twelve apostles. As John looks at this sight, what catches his eye is its "incredible wealth."

Remember, God is describing us as we will look to him in heaven. The wealth in the picture represents how valuable we are to God through faith in Jesus. John tells us the walls were made of jasper. The twelve foundations were each made of a precious stone and the twelve gates were each constructed of a single pearl. Even the streets were paved with gold. The opulence in this picture is the message. God is telling us that we will be *"rich toward God"* through faith in Jesus. God will see us as people of great value and we will live in his grace for eternity.

The angel in the vision now measures the city of God and in that act we discover another ancient connection to the promise of God. *The city was laid out like a square, as long as it was wide. He measured the city with the rod and found it to be 12,000 stadia in length, and as wide and high as it is long.* (Rev. 21:16 NIV) The city was shaped like a perfect cube. This shape calls to mind the ancient Temple Solomon built. At the heart of the Temple was a sacred room called "the Holy of Holies." The Holy of Holies was built at God's direction in the shape of a perfect cube. It was in the Holy of Holies that the nation of Israel through its High Priest met with God on one sacred day each year, the Day of Atonement. On that day the High Priest would enter into the presence of God with great caution. He would carry the blood of a sacrificed animal to atone for his sins and the sins of the people. He would wear bells on the bottom on his robe to alert the Lord to his coming so he would not die. Sinners entering into the presence of God did so at great peril to themselves. This is the ancient worship experience that stands behind the shape of the Holy City in this vision. God is telling us that the entire city in which all his children will live is now shaped in a cube like the Holy of Holies. The message is that there is no longer need for fear or for exclusion. No longer will we need a priest to enter into God's presence for us. All of God's children will now live and be welcomed into his presence in the fullness of joy for eternity.

There is one more ancient connection left for us to make as John finishes his description of the Holy City. John tells us the walls of the city were decorated with twelve rich jewels, reminding us of God's promises to his church. *The foundations of the city walls were decorated with every kind of precious stone.* (Rev. 21:19 NIV) Each of the twelve foundations was decorated with a different precious stone. John names the stones in order. As he recites the list of stones, our appreciation of the vision is deepened when we remember that the Old Testament High Priest wore an ancient breast piece decorated with twelve precious stones. Each of those stones contained the name of one of the tribes of Israel and the breast piece was worn by the priest over his heart. Now God uses those stones to decorate the foundations of the walls of his new holy and beautiful city. In heaven we will live close to God's heart each day, treasured by him.

John finishes the chapter by describing how living in the Holy City will be different from anything we have ever experienced. We will stand in the presence of God every day and he will welcome us as treasures to him. John highlights three main differences this makes in our experience. First he says there will be no temple or church. Churches have always been an integral part of the life experience of God's people while they walked this earth. The church was the place where God's people could enter into his presence and offer corporate worship. All that will change in the New Jerusalem. In that city God himself will live with us each day. We will always be in his presence.

A second difference is in the light of the city. *The city does not need the sun or the moon to shine on it, for the glory of God gives it light, and the Lamb is its lamp.* (Rev. 21:23 NIV) The New Testament pointed to Jesus as the *"light of the world."* In the New Jerusalem that prophecy will be fulfilled. The light of Jesus will illuminate the city. So great will be the light of the Lord that nations will walk by that light as they bring their gifts to honor the Lord for eternity.

The final difference John highlights is the character of the inhabitants of the city and the difference it makes. This might be the hardest difference to imagine. In a world that loves darkness, the children of God are always out of place. Worse than that, every effort to serve God is met in this world by ridicule and persecution from those who hate God and his light. How different it will be in the Holy City. There we will find an entire population united in the goal of serving God and living to please him. In that world the unbelievers will find no place. *The glory and honor of the nations will be brought into it. [27] Nothing impure will ever enter it, nor will anyone who does what is shameful or deceitful, but only those whose names are written in the Lamb's book of life.* (Rev. 21:26-27 NIV)

With that picture the vision draws to an end. There is but one last vision to see, perhaps the most important one of all. John told us that when the angel showed him the city God had prepared for us, the angel took John to a high mountain. The ancient prophet Isaiah spoke of that mountain in a vision long before and made a special promise to all mankind. *On this mountain he will destroy the shroud that enfolds all peoples, the sheet that covers all nations; [8]he will swallow up death forever. The Sovereign LORD will wipe away the tears from all faces; he will remove the disgrace of his people from all the earth.* (Isaiah 25:7,8 NIV) In the final chapter of the Revelation, God will leave us with a vision of that last and greatest promise fulfilled.

Read Revelation 22:1-20

The River and Tree of Life

And the Lord *God said, "The man has now become like one of us, knowing good and evil. He must not be allowed to reach out his hand and take also from the tree of life and eat, and live forever."* [23] *So the* Lord *God banished him from the Garden of Eden to work the ground from which he had been taken.* [24] *After he drove the man out, he placed on the east side of the Garden of Eden cherubim and a flaming sword flashing back and forth to guard the way to the tree of life.* (Genesis 3:22-24 NIV) Perhaps one of the saddest elements of the story of the first sin is the sight of the angel with the flaming sword guarding the tree of life. This tree represents the hopes and as-pirations of sinful man since that day. One after another the story of each human being ends with the same words, *"… and he died."* For all the centuries of human existence, families have carried the caskets of their dead to cemeteries. With hearts filled with sadness, looking through tear-filled eyes into the future, human beings have longed for the day when they could eat from the tree of life and the sad trail of death would come to an end. The Revelation makes it clear that God has the same goal in his heart. Throughout the years of human history God has been carrying out a plan to make that dream a reality. In this final chapter of the Revelation God speaks to all his children in the *"land of the shadow of death"* and tells us the tree of life is waiting for us. That is the story God tells with the final vision in this last chapter of the Bible.

As chapter twenty-two opens, we find ourselves still in the Holy City, the New Jerusalem. There John sees two amazing things. He sees a river flowing from the throne of God filled with the *"water of life."* On each side of this river John sees the tree of life bearing fruit each month. John notes that the leaves of this tree are for the *"healing of the nations."*

This vision, as we found with so many others in the Revelation, is rooted in a vision God gave to the ancient prophet Ezekiel. Ezekiel saw a river flowing from the Temple in Jerusalem and bringing life to other water that it touched and to the trees that lined its banks. God shows this same river and the tree of life it nourishes to John. The tree is planted in heaven and it bears fruit in great abundance, a new crop each month. Best of all, the fruit it bears is for everyone. No longer is mankind barred from eating. Now the fruit of life is available to all who stand with God in heaven.

The change that this tree will bring our future is almost beyond our ability to imagine. Every human being in this world has become so used to living with the daily reality of cemeteries and caskets and funerals and loss. Sin and its daily consequences seem so normal to us as we live in this world that we can hardly imagine life in their absence. Yet that is exactly the future God has prepared for us in heaven. God notes the parameters of this new life. *No longer will there be any curse. The throne of God and of the Lamb will be in the city, and his servants will serve him.* ⁴ *They will see his face, and his name will be on their foreheads.* ⁵ *There will be no more night. They will not need the light of a lamp or the light of the sun, for the Lord God will give them light. And they will reign forever and ever.* (Rev. 22:3-5 NIV) In heaven God will remove the curse of sin from our lives along with the terrible consequences of suffering and death that curse brought to us. The fruit of the tree of life will be our daily fare as we live each day with the shadow of death removed from our lives. Best of all the presence and favor of the Lord himself will be our daily joy. After a lifetime separated from God by sin, the children of God will stand in his presence every day, serving him in worship, and ruling with him for eternity. It is not called heaven for nothing!

God knows how these promises sound in our ears. For us a world filled with death is our normal experience. How hard it is for us to even imagine a world where death and the curse of sin do not exist. God knows our struggle. For this reason the Lord Jesus instructs his angel to emphasize the truth of his words as the vision comes to a close. *The angel said to me, "These words are trustworthy and true. The Lord, the God of the spirits of the prophets, sent his angel to show his servants the things that must soon take place."* (Rev. 22:6 NIV) These are the words of God himself. God is telling us to look past the hardship and the "normal" we see each day and to understand that a better future is waiting for us in heaven. In fact, it is closer than you think. That is the truth John hears next.

With the angel's final statement, this vision comes to an end. God has shown us all we need to see. The messages contained in the visions of the Revelation will equip us to live in this world and to accomplish the purpose God intends. But from the first vision, God has presented each new truth in the "shadow of urgency." That urgency becomes the primary focus now as God brings his message to a close. As it fades from view John hears the voice of the Savior himself speak words of promise. *Behold, I am coming soon! Blessed is he who keeps the words of the prophecy in this book.* (Rev. 22:7 NIV) These words are the focus on which each Christian should fix his attention every day he lives on this earth. The Lord is coming soon! Live ready! This promise of imminent return is the *"Revelation echo"* that guides the life of every child of God who has understood the visions and the message of the Revelation. This promise is our hope for each new day.

As John hears the voice of the Savior, he falls at the feet of the angel who brought him the vision. The angel recoils from John's misguided action and redirects his attention to God who has sent these visions. *"Worship God!"* Then the angel gives John an ominous command. *Then he told me, "Do not seal up the words of the prophecy of this book, because the time is near. ¹¹ Let him who does wrong continue to do wrong; let him who is vile continue to be vile; let him who does right continue to do right; and let him who is holy continue to be holy."* (Rev. 22:10-11 NIV)

God uses the visions of the Revelation to pull back the curtain revealing the spiritual war, a war which is responsible for all the things we see on the surface of life in this world. God has made his warning clear. But how people react to this warning is yet to be determined. Not all people will listen. The angel's ominous statement makes that point. The angel urges John to tell the world what he has seen and then let history take its course. Some will ignore God's warnings and continue to walk the path of darkness. They will face the consequences of God's judgment. Some will heed the warnings of God and live each day in the freedom Jesus won. But one day all will find themselves standing before the throne of the Lamb to give an answer for the lives they have lived.

This warning echoes in the final words of the Revelation. *Behold, I am coming soon! My reward is with me, and I will give to everyone according to what he has done.* (Rev. 22:12-16 NIV) Jesus is coming soon! Those who are ready will find his arrival to be a moment of great joy and blessing. But those who have not listened will find this moment to be one that ushers in permanent eternal despair and darkness. God wants all to share in his blessing. God wants all to be saved. So the Lord invites all to come and drink the water of life he has created. *The Spirit and the bride say, "Come!" And let him who hears say, "Come!" Whoever is thirsty, let him come; and whoever wishes, let him take the free gift of the water of life.* (Rev. 22:17 NIV)

This invitation brings with it one last warning regarding the book of Revelation and the visions it contains. As we walked through the challenging images presented in the Revelation, we have noted on numerous occasions that there are many people who love to bring their own imagination and their own reason to the study of this book. Some seem to view the visions of the Revelation as a challenge from God daring them to guess what the various details in the visions might mean. Far too often, the result of this speculation is not clarity but confusion. So common is this practice that, in the eyes of the world and even in the eyes of Christians, Revelation is a book so confusing no one can understand it. In that conclusion, the message of God is lost to people who vitally need to know what it says.

Nothing is more displeasing to God than those who dare to hide his message from people by substituting their own ideas. So to all who study this book, God issues a warning. *I warn everyone who hears the words of the prophecy of this book: If anyone adds anything to them, God will add to him the plagues described in this book. ¹⁹ And if anyone takes words away from this book of prophecy, God will take away from him his share in the tree of life and in the holy city, which are described in this book.* (Rev. 22:18,19 NIV) Do not add to what God is saying. God says what he means and he means what he says. Do not go beyond what God says and pass off your own words as the words of God. Those who ignore the warning of God will face the plagues described in the Revelation visions.

The second warning is equally strident. Do not remove anything from what God has said. Every truth God presents in the visions of the Revelation, and in the Bible in general, is necessary for God's children to know and to understand. Woe to the person who dares to take away even one of these truths from God's book. Those who subtract from God's word will lose their right to eat from the tree of life in heaven. With this warning God puts a usage label on the Revelation and on the Bible. That label reads, *"Word of God! Handle with care!"*

The Lord's message is now complete. He has prepared us to live in this world and to understand what we see. Jesus has given us a job to do. We are the lampstands of the Lord. He has warned us about the opposition we will encounter in a world that loves the darkness instead of the light, all the while needing that light more than anything else. The Lord revealed the huge spiritual war we are facing every day, a war that explains all the evil and the hardship we see. Finally, the Lord showed us how all this will come to an end with the defeat of his enemies and the reward to all who follow him.

Now Jesus himself speaks one last promise to our hearts as he closes the final pages of this book. And John leads us to respond with one last affirmation. *He who testifies to these things says, "Yes, I am coming soon." Amen. Come, Lord Jesus. [21] The grace of the Lord Jesus be with God's people. Amen.* (Rev. 22:20,21 NIV) It is my fervent hope and prayer that your study of the Revelation has proven to be a great blessing for you. I hope you have come to understand the seven messages God has presented on the pages of this book. Use these lessons each day to guide your steps. You are a lampstand for the Lord. The people in darkness around you need you to shine the light God gave you. Sharing the hope and confidence God has given you with the people around you will be the greatest joy you can find in life on this earth. And above all, live with your eyes fixed on the imminent return of the Lord. I look forward to meeting you in heaven at the end of our journey where together we will share in the reward that Jesus has revealed for all his people in the book of Revelation.

To God alone be the glory! Come Lord Jesus!

Summary

The Last Things, Part Two

In Revelation 21 and 22 God revealed the end he has prepared for his children. To do this God drew three pictures or visions of heaven. Each picture is drawn from God's perspective, showing us what heaven looks like through his eyes. Understanding this perspective is the key to learning what God is teaching in these pictures.

The Vision of the Bride of the Lamb *forms the first picture of heaven. On her wedding day, the husband sees his bride as the most beautiful she has ever been. This is the concept God captures with his vision of heaven. God is telling us in heaven we will appear to him as people of great beauty, like a bride on her wedding day. The source of our beauty will be the perfect life of Jesus Christ which we will wear as a robe. From this vision we learn that in heaven God will see us as favored and loved.*

The Vision of New Jerusalem *forms the second picture of heaven. God draws a picture of this city bedecked with jewels and filled with breathtaking wealth. God is telling us in heaven we will be "rich toward God." No news is more joyful than that for the sinner on this earth. Every day we live with a clear awareness that we are not what God created us to be. God has much reason to find fault in us. But in this vision God assures us in heaven all that will change. No more will we struggle with a sinful nature that loves sin. Sin and its curse will be removed from us forever. Perfection will be our reality. There God will see us as special treasures and he will be filled with joy whenever he looks at us.*

The Vision of the River of Life and the Tree of Life *forms the final picture of heaven. God uses this image to assure us that in heaven the shadow of death will be forever destroyed. Instead we will eat every day from the tree of life and we will be one with God for eternity.*

The Summary of the Seven Messages of the Revelation

The First Essential Revelation Truth -- *God's Purpose*

The Vision of Christ Among the Lampstands (Rev. 1)

Why does God allow the world to exist from one day to the next in the New Testament? God is sharing his message of light and hope through faith in Jesus with all people, before it is too late! When that work of light sharing is completed, the world will come to an end. This truth reveals our purpose as well. God gives us life each day so we can be lampstands for the Lord, touching as many people as we can every day with the hope and the confidence that come from the light of God.

The Second Essential Revelation Truth --
The "Lampstand Experience"

The Vision of the Seven Letters (Rev. 2-3)

The world needs God's light more than anything else if they are going to find hope in a world filled with despair. Yet in the Vision of the Seven Letters God reveals that the world will hate the light and those who bring it. The vision forms a "collage" of seven panels with each panel depicting a different experience that churches and Christians will have as they offer God's light to the darkness. Not all churches and not all Christians will have all seven experiences pictured in the collage. However, taken together, this collage forms a picture of the New Testament experience the lampstands of the Lord can expect to have. -- Note also that God paints "seven" panels. Using that number God is reminding us that, though the darkness will oppose and in some cases damage the lampstands, God will still use these flawed vessels to accomplish his important goal of reaching people with his light before it is too late!

The Third Essential Revelation Truth -- *Life will be hard for all people!*

The Vision of the Seven Seals (Rev. 4-6)
All people will suffer hardship in life due to the curse of sin. The terrible hardships form a message from God for unbelievers, warning the world of a greater judgment to come. Beside the normal struggles of life, believers will face the added burden of persecution from the world.

The Vision of the 144,000 Sealed by God (Rev. 7) -- *To reassure believers who are frightened by the sight of the hardships revealed under the seven seals, God reveals a picture of all believers on earth sealed by the Lord. God assures his people he will keep them safe as they walk through this dangerous world.*

The Vision of the White Robed Multitude (Rev. 7) -- *Continuing with pictures of reassurance, God reveals the future with his complete church safe at his side in heaven. We can be sure that God has already prepared victory for us and a sure future in heaven when our walk on earth is completed.*

The Fourth Essential Revelation Truth -- *Unbelievers will face God's wrath as they walk through life!*

The Vision of the Seven Trumpets of Judgment (Rev. 8-9)
The trumpets answer the question of Abraham, "Will you treat

believer and unbeliever the same?" God reveals that the unbeliever has a completely different experience from the believer as he walks through this world! The unbeliever experiences the wrath of God in every hardship. The believer never faces God's wrath, even when he faces hardship.

The Vision of the Mighty Angel (Rev. 10) -- *God revealed the Mighty Angel to assure his people that, in a world where the Trumpets of Judgment are blowing so loudly everyone will hear of God's wrath, the Mighty Angel will be so large and so loud that everyone will hear the Gospel of God's forgiveness in Christ as well.*

The Vision of the Measuring Rod (Rev. 11) -- *God tells us that while believers will see the visible church overrun with the darkness in this world (the outer court), God will still preserve his faithful people in the inner court who will carry his message into this world. The inner court does the work pictured by the Mighty Angel.*

The Vision of the Two Witnesses (Rev. 11) -- *The Two Witnesses, like the Mighty Angel, assure us that God's message of light and forgiveness through Jesus will be prominently displayed for the world to see until Jesus returns, even though the world objects.*

The Fifth Essential Revelation Truth -- *The Red Dragon is the evil spiritual cause of all suffering in this world! He is the enemy of mankind!*

The Vision of the Seven Visions (Rev. 12-15)
The Vision of the Seven Visions explains the cause of all suffering in this world. The injustice and pain and loss we see each day are the surface results of a spiritual war being fought between the forces of light and the forces of darkness. An

angry Red Dragon, along with his helpers, is fighting a spiritual war against God and his followers. This is the reason why evil things happen as they do in this world. The Vision of the Seven Visions tells us "why" the Black Horse and Red Horse and Pale Horse ride in this world.

The Vision of the Woman, the Child, and the Dragon (Rev. 12) -- *God uses this picture to reveal the spiritual war that lies beneath the surface of life in this world. This war is the cause of all suffering people encounter as the Red Dragon pours his wrath out on the world because he is filled with rage at his defeat by the forces of God.*

The Vision of the Beast of the Sea and the Beast of the Earth (Rev. 13) -- *God uses these frightening images to reveal that the Dragon will have two assistants in his attack on mankind. The devil will use anti-Christian government and anti-Christian religion as forces against God and his covenant plan.*

The Vision of the Lamb and the 144,000 (Rev. 14) -- *This picture of the people of God safe at his side in heaven is a comfort to Christians facing the Dragon and the beasts. It might appear that Christians cannot resist the power of these savage enemies, but God assures us that our victory is certain and our future at his side in heaven is secure.*

The Vision of the Three Angels (Rev. 14) -- *These three angels bring another message of assurance from God for his people as we walk this earth. The angels announce that the Gospel will continue to offer hope to all people even as the beasts and the Dragon rage. They announce that these powerful enemies will eventually be defeated. Their last proclamation assures us that those who follow the Dragon will be destroyed.*

The Vision of the Harvest (Rev. 14) -- *This vision offers one last message of comfort and assurance to God's people as* they live in a world plagued by strong spiritual enemies. On the last day God will bring his people safely to his side in heaven and send all who opposed him to an eternity of suffering in hell.

The Vision of Seven Angels with Seven Plagues (Rev. 15) -- *This is the last vision in the Vision of Seven Visions. God shows us a picture of seven angels coming from heaven carrying seven last plagues. With this picture God sets the stage to introduce the last things we need to understand to prepare us to live in this world. Having shown us what will happen and why it must happen, God will now begin to reveal how all things will come to an end.*

The Sixth Essential Revelation Truth -- *The End for God's Enemies (Revelation chapters 17-20)*

The Vision of the Seven Bowls of Wrath (Rev. 16)
God uses this vision to refocus our attention on the wrath God has reserved for those who walk in darkness. With this vision God begins to reveal the end he has planned for those who live opposed to his light.

The Vision of the Great Prostitute (Rev. 17) -- *God introduces a new enemy of the light who will help the Dragon and the beasts to advance the darkness in this world. In the end, God reveals that the Beast of the Sea will destroy this evil woman.*

The Vision of the Fall of Babylon (Rev. 18) -- *The world reacts to the demise of the Great Prostitute by mourning her destruction. In her sudden and rapid fall, the enemies of God sense a similar end might be waiting for them.*

The Vision of the Celebration in Heaven (Rev. 19) -- *While the world mourns the death of the Great Prostitute, the creatures of heaven celebrate her fall. Their joy increases when God* throws the Beast of the Sea and the False Prophet into the lake of burning sulfur.

The Vision of the Fall of the Dragon (Rev. 20) -- *After binding the Dragon for a thousand years, Satan is released to deceive the world one last time. This brings about the final battle between the forces of God and the forces of Satan. In the end God throws the Dragon into the lake of burning sulfur for eternity. All the enemies of God are defeated.*

The Seventh Essential Revelation Truth -- *The End God has Prepared for All Believers (Revelation chapters 21-22)*

The Three Visions of Heaven
God concludes the book of Revelation with three visions of heaven. In these visions God reveals the future he has prepared for the believers in eternity.

The Vision of the Bride of Christ -- *God pictures heaven as a beautiful bride on her wedding day. With this metaphor God shows us how believers will appear to God in heaven for eternity. God will find us "beautiful" in his sight, clothed with the robes of Christ's righteous life.*

The Vision of New Jerusalem -- *God pictures heaven as a rich city bedecked with jewels and gold. This image reveals that in heaven we will be "rich toward God" through faith in Jesus, valued by God as great treasures. That new "wealth" is a great comfort to sinful people who lived every day aware that in God's eyes, we were not what God created us to be.*

The Vision of the River of Life and the Tree of Life -- *In this vision a river filled with living water nourishes the tree of life from which the people of heaven eat daily. God promises eternal life in heaven as the believers eat from the tree of life and enjoy being in God's presence for eternity.*

Addendum

The Benefits Promised

You were promised three things at the onset of reading this book. Now that you have finished this task, please take some time to see if you have achieved what was promised.

Promise 1 -- *You will understand the visions of the Revelation and their message. In fact you will understand it so well that you can explain it to other people.*

Review the messages of each vision in the Revelation. With those messages in hand, you should be able to understand and explain what God is revealing in the Revelation without confusion or ambiguity.

Promise 2 -- *Armed with the messages God reveals in the Revelation, you will understand the events in the world around you. While others see only chaos on the surface of this earth, you will see and understand the plan of God.*

Apply the messages of the visions to the events you see happening in the world around you. These messages should explain why events in this world are happening. No longer should you be surprised at even the most terrible atrocities that occur each day, now that you know of the "Red Dragon" and his evil intentions.

Promise 3 -- *Equipped with the truth you learned in the visions of the Revelation, you will be able to live from this day on with confidence and hope.*

The messages God has revealed in the visions should fill

you with optimism as you face each new day. The world is a dangerous place and we are fighting a powerful spiritual enemy. However, God has assured us that we are "sealed" with his mark and he will protect us. Even better, what we see is temporary. God has prepared a sure and certain future for us at his side in heaven through faith in Jesus. Therefore, armed with these truths, we can live each day with hope in the face of every challenge. We know that God will turn all things into blessings for his people.

CPSIA information can be obtained at www.ICGtesting.com
Printed in the USA
LVOW12s1218150115

422930LV00001B/51/P

9 781478 733904